LAMBETH ESSAYS ON MINISTRY

Edited by
the Archbishop of Canterbury

Douglas Webster
Mollie Batten
James Mark
Leslie Houlden
Eric James
J. W. A. Howe
Alan Richardson
R. P. C. Hanson
Bernard Pawley

LAMBETH ESSAYS ON MINISTRY

PARALLEL VOLUMES

Lambeth Essays on Faith
Lambeth Essays on Unity

ALSO PUBLISHED BY S.P.C.K.

The Lambeth Conference 1968:
  Resolutions and Reports (with Seabury Press)
Lambeth Conference 1968: Preparatory Information

LAMBETH ESSAYS ON MINISTRY

Essays written for the Lambeth Conference 1968

Edited by the
Archbishop of Canterbury

LONDON S·P·C·K 1969

A selection from Lambeth Conference 1968: Preparatory Essays
produced by S.P.C.K. in 1968 for private circulation
First published in 1969
by S.P.C.K.
Holy Trinity Church, Marylebone Road, London N.W.1

Made and printed in Great Britain by
William Clowes and Sons, Limited, London and Beccles

SBN 281 02362 X

Contents

Notes on Contributors

The Reverend Canon D. Webster is Professor of Missions at Selly Oak Colleges, Birmingham.

Miss E. M. Batten, O.B.E., formerly Principal of William Temple College, Rugby, is Research Officer of the Board of Social Responsibility.

Mr J. Mark is on the staff of the Ministry of Overseas Development.

The Reverend J. L. Houlden is Fellow and Chaplain of Trinity College, Oxford.

The Reverend Canon E. James is Canon Residentiary of Southwark and Hon. Director of "Parish and People".

The Right Reverend J. W. A. Howe is Bishop of St Andrews, Dunkeld, and Dunblane, and has been appointed Anglican Executive Officer from May 1969.

The Very Reverend A. Richardson, formerly Professor of Theology at the University of Nottingham, is Dean of York Minster.

The Reverend Canon R. P. C. Hanson is Professor of Christian Theology at the University of Nottingham.

The Reverend Canon B. C. Pawley is Chancellor of Ely Cathedral.

Preface by
the Archbishop of Canterbury

The essays in this volume and its two companion volumes are among those which were written at my request for circulation to the bishops attending the Lambeth Conference of 1968 as part of the preparatory studies. Through the generous help of writers in different parts of the world some substantial material was produced under the headings of Faith, Ministry, and Unity.

I am sure that these three volumes will now be welcomed by a wider circle of readers in many Christian Churches. If the connection of the essays with the Lambeth Conference adds to their interest, I believe that their value lies in their role as independent considerations of some of the great issues which confront the Christian Church at this time.

MICHAEL CANTUAR:

1

Laymen in Mission

DOUGLAS WEBSTER

Two of the most significant changes in the Church of the twentieth century are the rediscovery of the meaning of laity and the reinterpretation of the meaning of mission. There is general recognition that *lay* can no longer imply amateur or second-class or unqualified and that *mission* can no longer be confined to the activities of missionary organizations and societies. Whereas the secular use—or misuse—of *lay* has to be resisted so that the biblical concept of the *laos*, the people of God, may again be understood, the secular use of mission should be duly noted because it has recaptured some of its biblical connotation which narrower ecclesiastical usage seems to have lost.[1]

The Lambeth Conference of 1958 pointed out that "too sharp a distinction has been made between clergy and laity. All baptized persons have the priestly vocation of offering life as a living sacrifice, acceptable to God through Jesus Christ. There is a ministry for every member of Christ; every man and woman who is confirmed is commissioned to this ministry in the Church, the home, the community, the world of business, and social life."[2] In the past the assumption has too often been that the clergy are those who minister and the laity are those who are ministered to. But in the New Testament ministry is understood primarily in terms of function rather than status. All Christians belong to the one people of God, all have some ministry to perform in the Body of Christ, and all have some share in the total mission of the Church in the world. Ministry is not to be confused with *the* ministry, that is the *ordained* ministry. A minority of the people of God are called and ordained to minister in special ways to the rest; their chief concerns are the Word, the sacraments, and pastoral care. But the people of God are concerned with serving him in the secular world. They do this by their daily work and witness and to this extent are involved in his mission. This is the ministry of the laity. It is in order that they may engage in this effectively that the

Church provides an ordained ministry to minister to them. By the same token it expects them to meet and express their corporate sense of belonging to the people of God in the ecclesia, the gathered congregation, that they may not fail to be the people of God in the diaspora, as they disperse as individuals into the world of work which is the sphere of mission. In this sphere the laity almost invariably exist as diaspora, like salt, like leaven.

It will be useful to trace briefly the development of the new concept of the laity. "Never in church history, since its initial period, has the role and responsibility of the laity in Church and world been a matter of so basic, systematic, comprehensive and intensive discussion in the total *oikoumenē* as today."[3] The truth of this statement is reflected not only in the reports of the first three Assemblies of the World Council of Churches but also in the massive volume of literature on this subject, much of it written since the last Lambeth Conference. The new factor in all this is not lay initiative; of that there was a great deal in the last two decades of the eighteenth century and the first half of the nineteenth. It is the theological awareness of the laity and their significance which is new. The seeds of this go back at least to 1937 and the Oxford Conference on Church, Community and State. In the preparatory volume for that conference J. H. Oldham, the first and perhaps the most influential of that new class of laymen in the full-time service of the world Church, wrote that "if the Christian faith is in the present and future to bring about changes, as it has done in the past, in the thought, habits and practices of society, it can only do this through being the living, working faith of multitudes of lay men and women conducting the ordinary affairs of life".[4]

In 1948 the first Assembly of the World Council of Churches at Amsterdam urged Churches to awaken to the importance of their lay members of both sexes, reminding them that the laity constitutes more than ninety-nine per cent of the Church. "Only by the witness of a spiritually intelligent and active laity can the Church *meet* the modern world in its actual perplexities and life situations."[5] The main significance of the lay member of the Church is not as a worker in the congregation but in the wider community. The second Assembly at Evanston in 1954 went further.

> The laity are not mere fragments of the Church who are scattered about in the world and who come together again for worship, instruction and specifically Christian fellowship on Sundays. They are Christ's representatives, no matter where they are. It is the laity who draw together

work and worship; it is they who bridge the gulf between the Church and the world, and it is they who manifest in word and action the Lordship of Christ over that world which claims so much of their time and energy and labour. This, and not some new order or organization, is the ministry of the laity . . . The time has come to make the ministry of the laity explicit, visible and active in the world. The real battles of the faith today are being fought in factories, shops, offices, and farms, in political parties and government agencies, in countless homes, in the press, radio and television, in the relationship of nations. Very often it is said that the Church should "go into these spheres"; but the fact is, that the Church is already in these spheres in the persons of its laity.[6]

The third Assembly at New Delhi in 1961 reaffirmed these basic convictions, wrestled with the definition of "laity", and—because the light of Christ is already shining in the world—saw the laity as "reflecting mirrors or focusing lenses, to beam the light into all parts of the world. Every Christian, carrying out his work as a ministry and using his particular gifts and the opportunities afforded to him, can bring the light of God's truth to bear in the world where he is, where dilemmas are faced and difficult decisions made."[7]

Parallel to this thinking in the World Council of Churches is a similar development in the Roman Catholic Church. There has been an emphasis on the lay apostolate, especially in the new missionary experiments in France since the end of the Second World War, though it has to be admitted that in some of the accounts of this one gets the impression that a *lay* apostolate is *faute de mieux*, hence the importance of the worker-priests. The Second Vatican Council not only issued a Decree on the Apostolate of the Laity but also gave a whole chapter to the laity in the Dogmatic Constitution on the Church. "The lay apostolate is a participation in the saving mission of the Church itself . . . Every layman, by virtue of the very gifts bestowed upon him, is at the same time a witness and a living instrument of the mission of the Church herself." One layman, commenting on this, remarked: "The lay apostolate has been simmering on the 'back burner' of the Church's apostolic life for nearly two thousand years, and finally the Fathers of this Council moved it up to the 'front burner' and turned the heat up all the way."[8]

The reasons for this new understanding of, and emphasis on, the laity are not far to seek. There has been the breaking up of Christendom and the *corpus Christianum* in Europe. Life is being increasingly secularized and the influence of bishops and clergy on public affairs accordingly diminished. There are vast areas of work and society from which the clergy are practically excluded. At the same time modern biblical scholarship has brought into the forefront of ecumenical thinking the image of the Church as God's people rather than as an hierarchical institution.

Thinking about mission has also been changing a good deal. In part this is a response to contemporary theology, in part it is a response to contemporary history. Until very recently the mission of the Church was almost entirely discharged (or thought to be) by specific mission-ary organizations. Often criticized their history is nevertheless a glorious one. Apart from these societies there might be no Anglican Communion, not to mention the expansion of other Churches by similar agencies. But one unfortunate result—though happily its worst manifestations are disappearing—has been an unbiblical dis-tinction between the Church and the mission. In many places the two existed side by side, related but separate. Now with the creation of provinces, the Anglican form of self-governing Churches, the mission has had to be integrated into the Church. Sometimes, alas, such integration has meant not merely the disappearance of *the* mission *qua* organization but the virtual death of the very notion of mission as a vital part of the Church's life. Churches are having to engage in mission without the help of *a* mission.

The second feature of our time is the exclusion of missionaries from certain countries or restrictions on their entry. China has closed its doors to foreign missionaries and according to a recent report only two churches remain open for regular Sunday worhip in the whole of China.[9] But this is not to say that the Christian mission in China has altogether come to an end, for mission is possible without mission-aries and without buildings. India, the world's second most populous country, is at the time of writing severely limiting its intake of mis-sionaries. In Malaysia a new law permits a maximum of ten years' service for each missionary. All this indicates the need to explore ways of mission which do not depend on professional missionaries.

Mission, however, is no longer thought of as a Western outreach to the rest of the world. On the one hand, mission has become a two-way traffic—and this in two respects. Christians from Asian countries have been sent by their Churches as missionaries to other Asian countries; some Africans have been missionaries in other African countries; it is reported that African students in Israel have had a pro-found missionary impact; and in Britain, North America, and Australia, there is increasing recognition of the missionary significance of Africans, Asians, and Latin Americans in our midst. But the West is now at the receiving end of other missionary movements, Muslim, Hindu, and Buddhist—hence the religious pluralism of this generation, enhanced by immigration and the multi-religious complexion of the student world in most universities. On the other hand, mission is now seen to be the operation of the Church in all six continents. The porch of every church building throughout the world opens on to a missionary situation. There is a local mission in every neighbourhood surrounding each Christian congregation, and to support "foreign" missions—or to depend on them—while neglecting mission on one's doorstep is to deny the very nature and purpose of the Church. The front-line of this local or neighbourhood mission is the laity. Every congregation should be structured for mission. Is this our aim?

A fourth factor to be reckoned with is that the Church can no longer count on having its own institutions in many countries. In the past there have been Christian schools and colleges and hospitals. These have belonged to the Church and have been the main thrust of its mission, the means of making contact with people and serving them. Those who have staffed these institutions have been employed by the Church even if they have not been missionaries. But the institutional phase of mission is already over or ending in most of Asia, and there is every reason to suppose that many African nations will follow the same course as soon as they can afford to do so, if not before. The Church will have to adapt itself to offering service in institutions which it can no longer control and which are not necessarily even Christian. It is unlikely that clergy will be acceptable even if they should be available and qualified to work in these. If there is to be mission in and through secular institutions, its agents will have to be laymen. It was at the Willingen Conference of the International Missionary Council in 1952 that the implications of all this for the Church were first set out by Canon Max Warren in a notable and prophetic address. He said:

I believe there is a call for an entirely new type of missionary activity to be developed alongside the traditional modes. We need, for instance, to envisage men and women of scientific training who will be ready to give their service in development schemes, going to their work as ordinary salaried officials and bringing their expert knowledge to bear on some local situations. But they will go, not merely as those whose Christian convictions are marginal to their work, as is commonly the case today.

Rather, they will go with a vocation consciously and deliberately to seek to work out a "disciplined and purified technology" in the light of Christian insights. Promotion and financial reward will, by such men, be completely subordinated to their Christian vocation. Others with the same dedication will go as experienced trade unionists, to help ensure that the young trade union movements of Africa and Asia are built up on Christian insights as to the meaning of society and the responsibility of individuals to society and of society to individuals. Yet others will bring a Christian integrity to the development of co-operative movements. These are just three illustrations.[10]

We have now reached a point where we can see the confluence of the two streams. The laity are clearly to be regarded as of the essence of the apostolate. At the same time, if there is to be mission in the future an increasing share of it will have to be borne not merely by laymen as distinct from clergy in the service of the Church, but by laymen seeing their work in the secular world as itself a missionary vocation. For, as Bishop Stephen Neill has pointed out, "If the Church is ever again to penetrate this alienated world and to claim it in the name of Christ, its only resources are in its convinced and converted laymen. There are vast areas, geographical and spiritual, which the ordained minister can hardly penetrate; the laymen are already there, and are there every day. What happens to society in the future will largely depend on the use that they make of their opportunities, of their effectiveness as Christian witnesses in a new and as yet imperfectly charted ocean of being."[11] Thus arises the concept: laymen in mission. What does it mean? What new problems does it create?

It may be wise to say at once what it does not mean. Laymen in mission does not mean ecclesiastical laymen doing work in the employment of the Church. Nor does it mean laymen acting as substitutes for clergy. Nor does it mean laymen working voluntarily for the Church by taking office as churchwardens, treasurers, sidesmen, stewards, lay readers, or members of the choir. Nor does it mean laymen conducting stewardship campaigns and the like. This is not to call in question the value of such work and the offices attached to those who do it, but merely to draw the necessary distinction between the Church doing its own household chores and the Church going out into the secular with its message and its willingness to serve.

"We preach not ourselves but Christ Jesus as Lord, and ourselves as your servants for Jesus' sake." In its worship the Church concentrates its attention on God and is helped to do this by those set apart for leading its liturgical activity. The Church exists supremely for God, to obey his first command and to love him above all else. But for that very reason the Church must exist for others and be world-centred too. This is the paradox of its nature because the first command does not stand alone, but is followed by the second to love our neighbours as ourselves. When modern theologians, such as H. Kraemer and J. C. Hoekendijk, urge the Church to be world-centred, they are not contrasting this with its being centred in God but with its being centred in itself. "The Church by being *world-centred* in the image of the divine example, is really the Church. Being Church-centred, regarding the world of the Church as the safe refuge from the world, is a betrayal of its nature and calling. Only by not being or not wanting to be an end in itself, the Church arrives at being the Church."[12] God sent his Son into the world, not into an ecclesiastical structure or institution which made no room for him, and in this world he lived as a layman by the norms of his day. His work was wholly for God and therefore wholly for the world, but it would be ludicrous to describe it as "church work".

Laymen in mission therefore means laymen in the world. They can be in the world in a manner which is impossible even for the most "worldly" clergy. Like most of their fellow men they earn their living in the world, and that is why they are there. But unlike most of their fellow men, because they are the people of God, *laymen*, they have other motives also, the chief of which are to bear witness to Christ and to serve in his Name. There would be many opinions about the best way of realizing these in secular situations. What then is the *mission* of such laymen?

In the first place it has to be recognized that work itself has value. Dr J. H. Oldham writing on this subject asks: "Why should a scientist or engineer or an administrator attach any great importance to religion unless it says to him: 'In the work you are doing day by day you are a partner of God in his work of creation and the realization of his purpose for the family of the sons of men'."[13] Failure to see this or to acquire thorough competence in one's secular calling, or to use it simply as a platform for propagating Christianity is as reprehensible for Christians as for Marxists. The witness of the majority of laymen is given by bringing integrity, conscientiousness, and dedication to their job and by establishing good relationships with it. The ease with which so many people "talk shop" is an indication of this dedication. A layman has pointed out that most Christians are in fact more at home in the secular world than in the Church and find more fellowship at work than in the pew. It is not being suggested that honest work is itself mission, for there are plenty of non-Christians with high moral standards in this respect. But such an attitude to work is an essential condition and prerequisite for laymen in mission.

Secondly, while conspicuousness is usually undesirable, at some points and in some sense laymen must be prepared to be visible Christians in the secular world. "For years talking about the laity has meant talking about their place in the Church gathered for worship, instruction and government: now it means talking about their calling to be the Church in the world."[14] There are situations where the Church can be hidden and its members incognito, but there are others where they must be seen and heard.

A prominent Christian layman says that the layman's job is to be a pioneer.[15] It has already been noted in passing that towards the end of the eighteenth century laymen took a prominent part in pioneering the formation of the great missionary societies. The Clapham Sect was entirely lay except for John Venn, their rector. Few groups in history have had a greater effect on their own and successive generations. The High Church party also had laymen who in fellowship with others pioneered. In many parts of the world the Church was founded not by missionaries or clergy but by laymen who were there under secular auspices. It is well known that the Church in parts of the Punjab and the North-West Frontier of the Indian sub-continent came into being through the witness of officers in the British Army. In countless African towns and villages the first Christian was not a missionary but a trader who had come from some other town and brought his faith with him, founding a church in his house.

A fourth point to notice is the positive advantage laymen have in mission over against clergy. The fact that they are not paid to promote Christianity and are not therefore "professionals" is of immense significance. Among their fellow men, that reason alone will give them an influence denied to most clergy by virtue of their different vocation. This advantage, however, belongs to secular laymen in the world and not to ecclesiastical laymen, such as catechists and others, whose full-time employment is with the Church. There are areas of the world, for example the oil fields of the Arabian-Persian gulf, where no increase in the number of clergy or missionaries would materially affect the Christian mission. The one thing needful is laymen, convinced and converted, ready to be "salty Christians".

It is almost forty years since Roland Allen published privately an essay on "Non-Professional Missionaries".[16] This idea is now coming into its own. Roland Allen may have overstated his case, but at least there is a case to state. Today the ground of criticism of the official missionary bodies has shifted, but the need for mission and missionaries outside them is infinitely greater. The general secretary of one society has put it like this: "It is partly a problem of inverted commas: how to be a missionary in the full sense of the word without being a 'missionary'." The same writer explains what he means by reference to the attitude of the modern young.

> One aspect of secularization . . . is the preference for getting on with the immediate technical job—building a dam, discovering a vaccine, teaching a class—without offering any religious or ideological reason for doing so . . . This *ad hoc* response is the only kind of obedience which rings true to many of the liveliest young Christians today. They will give themselves to meet a need without reserve but also without pretensions. They will serve but without a label. A call makes sense to them but not a vocation. The only response they can make with integrity is in such terms as "I will go now; who knows what will happen next year?" "I can give one tour; how can I tell what the opening will be after that?"[17]

One result of this mood is a greater number of young people offering many kinds of service for short spells of up to two years outside their own country than ever before. Two of the best-known organizations for this are the Peace Corps and Voluntary Service Overseas. There are others. Those who go out as Christians under these auspices are laymen in mission, whether they know it or not. D. T. Niles tells how once he met a young American going to teach English in one of the high schools of Ceylon. The youth asked him whether there was anything he could tell him that would help his work in Ceylon. "I said to him, 'There is one thing you must remember—that you will always be judged as a Christian missionary'. He looked startled, 'But I am not a missionary', he said. 'I am simply going to teach English.' I said to him, 'That makes no difference. You will be judged as a missionary. You in the West who bear the name of Christ can discount responsibility for it in your own countries, but abroad it is the Name by which you will be judged'."[18]

In addition to young people doing various kinds of voluntary work there are without exception ex-patriates in every country of the world. There are the business and banking communities in most great cities, the staffs of international airlines, the diplomatic corps, technical aid teams, teachers in universities, doctors and nurses in hospitals, members of the armed services in certain countries, tourists, visiting sports teams, entertainers, and artists. There are hundreds of thousands of students. There are immigrants. This is not a one-way traffic from the West to Africa and the East. Something of the brain drain suffered by Asia is to be seen in the number of Indian doctors in British hospitals. The London Transport system, not to mention others, might come to a halt but for the men and women from the West Indies. Many British factories depend to a great extent on labour from overseas. The Chinese dispersion is not limited to South-East Asia, for there are Chinese restaurants in most cities of any size, even in West Africa. Indian migrants are to be found not only in Singapore and Malaya but also in Fiji, Honolulu, and Trinidad, and in East and West Africa. Some form of American presence is almost universal. In all these groups it can be assumed that there are Christians and in certain groups there are many. The problem is to help them to relate their residence and work in a particular country, not their own, to the mission of the Church in that place. Many of these could be non-professional missionaries or laymen in mission.

One British missionary society has already laid plans for experimenting with the idea of secular missionaries. It goes without saying that these would have to be laymen. It recognizes that there must still be missionaries

> who go out in response to the call of a diocese or church institution and put themselves at its disposal. There will be those who share in ecumenical ventures outside any one ecclesiastical jurisdiction. Others, again, will be under contract to governments or universities or commercial firms, yet engaged just as deliberately in the mission of the Church as any of its paid workers. And in special situations there may be missionaries unknown as such by anyone else in the area. Each of these, whether church-worker or strictly lay and "secular", must see himself as part of the outreach of the local church. For the word "missionary" does not describe a separate profession among other professions, but, rather, an underlying life-purpose in the pursuit of which a person has gone from his own country or his own *milieu* to another.[19]

All this indicates the great potential for mission available in the laity, given an understanding of what mission means and what being a lay person means. If the Church is to make use of this potential, it must face up to a new educational task and a new pastoral task. This double task has to be carried on at both the sending and the receiving ends, for we have seen that the flow is in each direction. Basically the educational task must be undertaken by sending Churches, the pastoral by receiving Churches. Put another way this means that we have responsibility for training those who go from us and for giving pastoral care to those who come to us, wherever "we" may be and wherever "they" come from.

What are the main elements in any educational programme? How must they be carried out? Clearly the foundations for any such programme are an adequate understanding of the two concepts of laity and mission. Regular teaching on these lines needs to be given not merely at special conferences but in local churches on ordinary occasions. It should be part of the Church's teaching programme for children, youth, and confirmation classes. It should be a subject discussed from time to time at parish meetings and church councils. As with most things the seeds must be sown in the local church, but with this in view central bodies with a qualified staff should provide resource material and study outlines. In professions or areas where men and women are constantly going overseas efforts should be made to use such courses as are available—even if they are not run by Christian agencies—or to provide them where they are lacking. They should include an introduction to the history, culture, and religion of another people, a facing up to the problem of "culture shock" and any hidden complexes about colour or racial superiority. Let it be emphasized again that this needs doing both ways not only for Europeans and Americans setting out for developing countries but for Africans, Asians, and Latin Americans going to the West. A number of such courses in the West are described by Dr Paul Löffler.[20] The West has more facilities for running them. But on however small or brief a scale similar preparation is desperately urgent outside the West for those coming into its orbit. A Jamaican Christian driving a London bus or an Indian Christian working in a Birmingham foundry is as much a layman in mission as an English professor at an African university or a Canadian technician working for the World Health Organization in Pakistan.

At the time of writing this essay a two-year research project sponsored by the Conference of Missionary Societies in Great Britain and Ireland is being carried out on Laymen Abroad in Christian Mission. Among the interim conclusions so far made available are the following.[21] The role of the layman abroad in secular occupation with a missionary intention, though grasped by some of our church and missionary leaders, is far from being an integral part of the thinking and teaching of the Church in Britain. The vision has yet to break through into wider circles. The paramount need for Christian laymen overseas is admitted, but very few of the thousands who go abroad have any sense of a need for religious preparation. There is no one organization to promote this challenge. On the whole, government departments show a willingness to co-operate, but business and industry are very cautious about having direct dealings with church organizations except at a personal and unofficial level. The researcher recommends the establishment of a Bureau to promote this vocation, to distribute information, and to co-ordinate the work of the various interested bodies.

In all planning about the Christian mission desirable ideals must not blind us to responsible realism. It would be an immense achieve-ment if a larger number of Christians in their home churches under-stood that part of their vocation is to be a witness for Jesus Christ. While we fall so far short of this aim, it is hardly practical to expect every Christian going overseas to understand what is meant by mis-sion and to take a share in it. If something worth while can be done among only a small minority of the thousands going abroad each year, this would be a cause for hope. It is better to begin on a small scale with a pilot project—as did the founders of the missionary societies—than to launch a large organization which proves to be hollow or premature. In this life little is accomplished by organized bodies until there is a sufficiently powerful spirit to make them come alive. It is easy enough to start an organization if funds become avail-able, but this alone does not ensure its goals being reached. Neverthe-less this raises questions which deserve thorough investigation and discussion. It cannot be doubted that some kind of special training is necessary for the few; what has to be decided is how and where this can best be given.

Of equal importance and urgency is the pastoral consideration. Everyone in a country other than his own is exposed to special prob-lems and sometimes strains. Many are homesick; some are lonely; a few develop behaviour patterns which they would not follow at home. It is easy to be insensitive to a community when one is an alien in it. It is easier still to restrict relationships to the apparent safety and familiarity of one's own countrymen and to enjoy the amenities of a club or clique or colony. Making friendships across cultural and linguistic, let alone religious, barriers can be difficult and not without risks of misunderstanding and pain, as any reader of E. M. Forster's *A Passage to India* will appreciate. A more modern presentation of this will be found in *The Ugly American* by William Lederer and Eugene Burdick. The characters in these two books were laymen abroad but hardly on mission. Beside their need of a fuller preparation was their yet more pressing need of adequate pastoral care. Unless laymen abroad can make real relationships, they cannot engage in Christian mission, and it is doubtful whether they can be truly effective in their secular occupation. Many Europeans still go to Africa or Asia with a false stereotype image of the Negro or the Oriental character, based on assumptions or gossip uncritically accepted. There is evidence that the same can be true in reverse. It is a matter for sad reflection that of the West Indian migrants living in London, whereas sixty-nine per cent used to attend churches in the West Indies only four per cent attend churches in London. Brought up to look on England with affection as the "Mother Country" they "speak of their shock and bewilderment upon discovering that England was not the Mecca of Christianity that they had always believed. There can be no doubt at all that this is a major cause of many migrants' lapse of faith. This experience is for most of them a bitter pill to swallow. It is like discovering that one's mother is a liar and a hypocrite." [22] At both ends Churches are culpable in this respect. In the West Indies there should be far more briefing about what to expect, and in Britain there should be far more patience and pastoral understanding. But this is only one example of the enormous demands made upon the Church pastorally by laymen abroad. Unless the Church can meet their pastoral needs, these laymen will be utterly ineffective in terms of mission.

The same applies in reverse to Europeans and Americans in Africa, Asia, and Latin America. Certainly it is their duty as Christians to join up with the local church and share in its activity, even if there is a language barrier. But great responsibility rests upon the local church and its ministers to offer them the right hand of fellowship and to give them pastoral care. Where for linguistic or other reasons— as in the case of Chinese seamen in the Port of London—nationals cannot give this care to expatriates in their midst, some kind of chaplaincy service should be provided. The danger of chaplaincy churches is that they will inhibit adventurous relationships with indigenous Christians and prevent any deep contact with their worshipping and witnessing communities, not to mention participation in them. Yet these risks are less than those of losing faith as a result of pastoral neglect. Where chaplains to foreign communities are deemed necessary, every effort should be made mutually by themselves and the Church of the country to see that neither they nor their congregations are isolated.

Considerable attention has been given to the pastoral care of missionaries. Happily, in an increasing number of dioceses, there are bishops, clergy, or mature lay people who can exercise this in a responsible way. But for various reasons this is still not the case everywhere. In such circumstances the sending Church or society has to make special provision for the spiritual needs of its missionaries, and the sense of belonging to a community with its own depth of mutual commitment and discipline can be a great strength. This has always been the practice and experience of the religious communities and partly accounts for their survival. It has been urged that similar forms of community, such as a third order, or an association with a rule of life, would be of great benefit to many laymen engaged in mission in the secular world. No one single association would be able to meet the varied needs of all, but there is obviously room for a number of such fellowships. Some exist already. More are needed.

This essay has attempted to bring together and to summarize some of the thinking on its subject which has been made available since the last Lambeth Conference. Its purpose has not been to reach conclusions but to raise questions. There are many issues deserving further consideration, but we do not start from scratch. Both at the ecumenical level and among some of our Anglican leaders distinguished contributions have been made and should be studied. It is hoped that the references and the bibliography will provide a measure of resource material.

The present writer has been deeply aware of one disadvantage in fulfilling the request to write these pages. He is not a layman earning his living in the secular world. The bishops who consider this subject at Lambeth will be in the same position. What has been written is offered, bearing in mind all the way through that "the laity are not the helpers of the clergy so that the clergy can do their job, but the clergy are helpers of the whole people of God, so that the laity can be the Church".[23] Where the clergy remember this and the laity are equipped for their mission, one discovery is made sooner or later: far from being irrelevant, theology (and the theologian) become indispensable. For in the last analysis mission is concerned with sharing the gospel and theology with understanding it.

NOTES

1. See Max Warren, "That Curious Word 'Missionary'" in *Frontier*, Winter 1965/6.
2. Lambeth Conference 1958 Report, 1.26.
3. H. Kraemer, quoted by Hans-Ruedi Weber, *The Layman in Christian History*, p. 377.
4. K. Bliss, *We the People*, p. 59.
5. The First Assembly of the World Council of Churches: Official Report, pp. 153–6.
6. The Evanston Report, pp. 161, 168.
7. The New Delhi Report, p. 203.
8. The Documents of Vatican II, ed. Walter M. Abbott, s.j. (Geoffrey Chapman, 1966), pp. 60, 476.
9. *Church Times*, 7 July 1967.
10. Max Warren in *Missions under the Cross*, ed. Norman Goodall (Edinburgh House Press, 1953), p. 31.
11. S. C. Neill, *The Layman in Christian History*, p. 22.
12. H. Kraemer, *A Theology of the Laity*, p. 130.
13. J. H. Oldham, *Life is Commitment* (S.C.M. Press, 1963), p. 100.
14. K. Bliss, op. cit., p. 29.
15. K. G. Grubb, *A Layman Looks at the Church*, pp. 21, 30, 35.
16. D. M. Paton (ed.), *The Ministry of the Spirit*. Commented on by Paul Löffler, *The Layman Abroad in the Mission of the Church*, pp. 21ff.
17. John V. Taylor, C.M.S. News-Letter, January 1966.
18. D. T. Niles, *Upon the Earth* (Lutterworth, 1962), p. 195.
19. John V. Taylor, C.M.S. News-Letter, February 1966.
20. Paul Löffler, op. cit., pp. 40ff.
21. Ian Thomson. See short bibliography.
22. Clifford S. Hill, *West Indian Migrants and the London Churches* (O.U.P., 1963), pp. 5f, 19f.
23. Hans-Ruedi Weber, quoted by J. A. T. Robinson, *The New Reformation?* (S.C.M. Press, 1965), p. 55.

SHORT BIBLIOGRAPHY

Stephen C. Neill and Hans-Ruedi Weber (ed.), *The Laymen in Christian History*. S.C.M. Press, 1963.

Yves M. J. Congar, o.p., *Lay People in the Church*. Geoffrey Chapman, 1959.

Hendrik Kraemer, *A Theology of the Laity*. Lutterworth, 1958.

J. A. T. Robinson and others, *Layman's Church*. Lutterworth. 1963.

Kathleen Bliss, *We the People*. S.C.M. Press, 1963.

Kenneth G. Grubb, *A Layman Looks at the Church*. Hodder and Stoughton, 1964.

Mark Gibbs and T. Ralph Morton, *God's Frozen People*. Fontana (Collins), 1964.

J. C. Hoekendijk, *The Church Inside Out*. S.C.M. Press, 1967.

Horst Symanowski, *The Christian Witness in an Industrial Society*. Collins, 1966.

Paul Löffler, *The Layman Abroad in the Mission of the Church*. Edinburgh House Press, 1962.

D. M. Paton (ed.), *The Ministry of the Spirit*. (Selected Writings of Roland Allen.) World Dominion Press, 1960.

Ian Thomson, *Laymen Abroad in Christian Mission*. Cyclostyled Interim Report 1967, available from Conference of Missionary Societies of Great Britain and Ireland.

"Laymen Abroad", an article in *International Review of Missions*, Vol. LVI, No. 224 (October 1967). This article contains the Final Group Reports at the World Consultation on "Laymen Abroad", Loccum, Germany, 10–16 June 1967.

2

Laymen in Society

MOLLIE BATTEN

During recent decades changes in the thought and life of peoples and Churches all over the world have led to the debate about the place and tasks of the laity. To what extent new ideas have led to changes in practice may well be asked since, in all human affairs, changes will be welcomed by some and resisted by others. But the reaffirmation of the biblical understanding of the Church as the whole People of God, the Laos, has now become an assumption of the discussion.[1] Attempts are now being made to work out more precisely the meaning of the ministries of clergy and laity in relation to one another within the total Laos. The purpose of this essay is to explore further what this new view of the laity, or lay men and women, implies for their ministry in society, or, to use the title of an early book by Dr J. A. T. Robinson "On being the Church in the World".[2]

There are, of course, church people today, as there always have been, who believe, even if they do not say so, that the Church is a religious society existing for the benefit of religious people. Both the Old Israel and the New Israel in biblical times found it difficult to break through from the notion of election for salvation to the idea of election for service. The belief that God is concerned that a limited number of people should be saved out of this wicked world into the Church, in order to achieve a blessed life hereafter, persists among Christians and, unfortunately, among many who are critical of the Church because Christians are thought to believe this. If this view or anything like it is true there is no need for this essay, there is no ministry of laymen in society because God is not concerned about society and the laymen should not be either. They may occasionally give alms, but even these are best given to those "who are of the household of faith"!

Perhaps a more commonly held view is that the task of clergy and laity is to build up the Church by missionary activity to individuals in

personal terms regardless of their social circumstances and responsibilities. If and when sufficient individuals are saved into the Church,
so this argument goes, society will then be saved because society is
simply a collection of individuals. If each individual knows his personal Christian duty, that is all that is needed for the advancement of
the Kingdom of God, here and hereafter. It is possible to quote the
Bible and much Christian tradition in support of this view. Churches
today in their weakness, confronted by secular affluence or hostile
governments or by the sheer weight of numbers of people who have
never heard the gospel, may well feel this to be their primary, if not
their sole, task. But, if this be true, there is no need for this essay, for
such a view implies that God's concern is with individuals apart from
society; society is nothing but a collection of them. It will, however,
be argued in this essay that this is a very limited insight into the
understanding of God and man, rooted in the Bible and the Christian
tradition. It also ignores modern social studies and our awareness
that human beings live in, influence, and are influenced by the large-
scale, complex, and powerful institutions and associations of modern
would-be democratic society.

Yet another view is represented by the interpretation of the
ministry of laymen in society as service or *diakonia*. In various ways,
in different societies in the world today, the family, even where the
extended kinship group is still a reality, is insufficient to meet all the
needs of the young and the old, the sick and the inadequate. Communities are too fragmented for this to be possible and new knowledge and skills demand that there shall be specialized services and
institutions to provide the means of caring and healing now available.
Governments, nationally and locally, as well as voluntary bodies,
step in to supplement family and individual care. Christians are
rightly distressed at human need and feel compelled to take part in
these new social services, as professionals or as volunteers. Their
biblical warrant is found in Deuteronomy, in the parable of the Good
Samaritan, in James 1.27. There is a great Christian tradition of
identifying with the poor and the sick and the ignorant and ministering
to them. This is what is frequently meant by the ministry of laymen
in society.[3] It is certainly an important part of "Being the Church in
the World", of expressing the gospel in existence and activity as well
as in word. But the holders of this view may assume that God is at
work in society solely through the Church and that the ministry of
laymen in society can be carried out while they accept society as it is.

Some also believe that such activity by laymen is somehow "different" from similar work undertaken by non-Christians. This, it will be urged in this essay, is still inadequate to the truth of God's purposes for, and concern with, the whole world and his activity through all human service. The laymen's ministry is not only *in* society, but *with*, *for*, and *to* society.

What then is the thesis of this essay? It depends upon the view that modern biblical and theological scholarship related to contemporary scientific and historical studies have confirmed and clarified certain insights into the being, purposes, concerns, and activities of God in relation to the world as well as to the Church. This view has been put forward at greater length by Dr L. Hodgson[4] and others. This is not the place to defend this view nor to consider the challenges to it both intellectual and social. It is proposed to spell it out and to make plain certain implications of it. For, if laymen are to minister *in* and *to* society, as it is believed they should, the organized Churches as well as laymen must understand this view for themselves and for their ministry.

It is perhaps right to pause at this point to indicate what is meant by "laymen" in this context. The notion will not mean ecclesiastically minded laity who hold any of the views we have already rejected as mistaken or inadequate. Nor will it mean the many people who turn to the organized Churches today because they have need for a welcoming community in their inability to find that for themselves elsewhere, maybe because they are sick in body or mind, or socially insufficient to their circumstances. They need and must have care, and are not able to go on active service. "Laymen", for the purpose of this essay, will include all those men and women who are capable of being active and who, in some way or another, hold what they believe Christians to hold and who would say that they are, in some sense, motivated by Christian ideals. They may have been educated in a Christian school or college; they may have read the New Testament as literature; they may or may not be informed or articulate about their faith. They may or may not be associated with a local Christian congregation. They also vary enormously in capabilities, interests, and responsibilities. They are scattered throughout the social structures of modern societies, some as decision-makers, some as opinion-formers, and many as quite ordinary folk who will follow where they think truth leads them. Many of them are confused about their ministry in and to society.

It will now be argued that they should regard their ministry, and be helped to regard it, on the basis of Christian beliefs in these ways:

1. God is the living, loving God who is the source of all being, power, and activity. He is continually creating and sustaining all that is. All science (what we know of this universe) and all technology (how we do things), all sources of physical power and all material things are his good gifts so that mankind may make a framework in which full human potential may be realized. God is, therefore, concerned about all human life, and all activity takes place within his activity as human beings organize their political and economic institutions, their cities, towns, and villages. He is ultimately responsible for their on-going existence and the productivity of every factory, shop, office, and mine. He is the source of the life of all human beings as neighbours and members of families.

2. God made man and gave him his human potentialities, including reason and some freedom and some free will; man has a unique place in creation and has some power over it. His achievements are amazing and he now is able, in co-operation with God, by work, knowledge, and skill to overcome scarcity and to be fruitful in every respect. Thus he is able to provide all that mankind needs to live to the full a balanced life of work and leisure and rest.[5]

3. Such beliefs in the goodness of God and man are difficult today and they are made more difficult because of the mystery of evil. The old theological words are of little use in this area of thought. Men are as aware of corporate ills and sufferings as of their individual failures. They are appalled that all human life is lived under a balance of terror. They are guilty and afraid and revolted because of man's inhumanity to man. Men feel isolated and alienated in countless ways —in fragmented societies, played upon by the mass media. They feel lost in large-scale and powerful political and economic institutions in which there are racial riots, class conflicts, and much individual selfishness. Men cry out in anguish against God and their fellow men, or they find life trivial and absurd. Laymen in society will continually be faced by doubts and fears as they feel these things upon their pulses. Each of them will be led, over and over again, to ask: What can it all mean? Can I really go on believing even the things about God and man which I try to believe?

4. But Christians believe that God has taken steps to deal with the state of his world. He has identified himself with it in the life, death, and rising again of Jesus Christ. In him God's forgiveness of man is made plain and effective. Because he, *the* man, lived and died as he did and triumphed over death, men can respond in faith and repentance, and accept that forgiveness, and forgive one another. From this springs new life—for individuals and for societies. Only by such love, suffering, compassion, forgiveness, and starting again can any redemption and reconciliation take place in Church or in society. Whenever redemption and reconciliation take place it is God's work in Christ Jesus—whether men know it or not, or name his name or not. Laymen need to believe this about all changes for the better wrought out at cost by individuals or societies. Many men of good will the world over today regard Jesus as a good man or even as a prophet. But they do not recognize, and they are reluctant to be involved in, the costly activity of redemption and reconciliation in God's world. They do not understand that wherever and whenever that costly process is at work in society—as well as in individuals— the Christ is incarnate again and the cross and the glory are taking place eternally.

5. Theologically, to describe the work of God the Father and Son thus at work in the world and in the Church is to set forth the work of God the Holy Spirit. Many laymen are as confused as many ecclesiastics are about God the Holy Spirit. They use mechanical or physical rather than personal analogies and they believe that the Holy Spirit comes in as "an extra" when they have completed their studies of a situation and have to decide and act to the best of their ability. But Christians pray that the Holy Spirit will give them a right judgement in all things. On the view here being argued, God the Holy Spirit is at work in all men who, with singleness of mind and integrity of purpose, try to discern the truth of things *as* they patiently study the facts of the case, *as* they weigh up the alternatives, and *as* they judge and decide and act.

6. In all societies today values, laws, moral judgements, and ethical reflections are being questioned. Christians are too apt to "moan about morals". But in such swiftly changing circumstances judgements must change as the Holy Spirit leads into new truth. Laymen, and indeed all churchmen, have to learn to examine new judgements and behaviour so that they may hold fast only that which is good and

go forward with courage into new insights—for the healthy life of social and economic institutions, the power-structures and the complex organizations of human associations of the modern world, as well as for individuals. Laymen and other good men in all societies need much more help in these matters. More will be written about this later.[6] Laymen also need to understand, to desire, and to use power. The Gospels have been searched with the word "poverty" in mind. They need to be looked at anew in the light of our notions of authority and power. There is much there to support the view that the important thing about power, as about bread, is to have enough of it and to use it rightly to the glory of God and in the service of man.

As laymen decide and act, day by day, they will believe that sometimes they are right and sometimes they are wrong. They have to learn to understand that life has to be lived in faith; no man can ever be sure about God's will in a situation. They need to be encouraged to go on faithfully deciding and acting. "Much evil is done when good men do nothing" and "not to decide is to decide not". The right will be seen as that which is more good and less evil, and the wrong will be that which appears more evil and less good. They will always have doubts, and their consciences will be troubled especially in grave matters which involve many people and resources over long periods of time. They need continually to be reassured that they are forgiven sinners and that God's goodness and grace are still at work—in every human situation however difficult or distressing. New opportunities and initiatives are always possible. In this way laymen in their ministry in and to society share the cross, they exercise their priesthood in the world. They can go on in faith, courage, and hope.

7. Their beliefs about God and man and life in this universe are inevitably associated with questions about death and judgement. Laymen are deeply baffled about these ultimate human concerns, not least because they feel that Churches and churchmen are hesitant, confused, and inarticulate about them. Whatever images churchmen may have of the life hereafter it is surely true in history that only as and when life in this world is seen to be important and valuable because of God's continuing care for all men that life hereafter is held to be important and necessary. The New Testament is about new life, eternal life, here and now as a foretaste of the fulfilment of that life hereafter.

So far we have been describing the beliefs and the implications of those beliefs which Christians hope will inform, and increasingly be understood by, the many varieties of laymen we have envisaged as exercising a ministry in and to society. They have been called "laymen incognito". Their ministry is exercised in and through their being and activity wherever they are undertaking their everyday tasks in all the organized life of the contemporary world.

What then, it may be asked, is the special nature and ministry of the Church, that is of the organized Churches, and of those laymen who definitely profess and call themselves Christians? When the word Christian is used they are prepared to stand up and be counted. They are the called-out people of God. They are called out corporately and individually to express (by all their purposes, concerns, and activities) the very life and being of God as they seek after his purposes, concerns, and activities in his world. This is their sacramental task which is focused in the sacraments. The Christian Church should be a demonstration in society of what society should be like. The "style of life" of the consciously Christian layman should reflect the life of society today; he will be a secular man living a Christ-like life in the contemporary world. Much of the time, the Christian laymen we have in mind will exist and act in the world incognito as the other varieties of laymen we have described. They should be motivated by their beliefs and their judgements and activities should be based upon them; these will express their meaning and purpose and much of the time that will be their ministry. Only from time to time, in dialogue with their fellow men, will laymen who are professing Christians be asked to explain what they do, and then they will speak of their motives and judgements as they are informed by their beliefs. They will respect the secular and pluralistic societies in which they work and the rights of all men to their convictions. They will not therefore seek to abuse professional position or the possession of power or status of any kind in order to press their convictions on fellow men. But sometimes these laymen who are avowed Christians may be asked about their beliefs and then, if they are lively *and* informed *and* articulate, they will be able to witness to their faith and its interpretation of all man's life in every aspect of society.

What about all the laymen incognito who would hesitate to profess and call themselves Christians? What about their worship and prayer? They find it difficult to speak about this. Many of them will not be at home in existing local congregations for all sorts of reasons.

They must not be judged to be proud or perverse; many of them have reasons which to them are honest and sincere. But who knows when such laymen in their life and work in society will find themselves expressing their praise and thanks to God for his goodness and grace? Who can say when, as they are involved in the conflicts and confusions of life and have to decide and act, they may turn to the-power-of-all-that-is for forgiveness and courage and hope? Who can tell when the sheer needs of the world as they experience them, and their own inadequacies, may lead them to some kind of intercession and petition, for others as well as for themselves? No one knows—and Christians need great sensitivity and understanding if such stirrings in these experiences of men in the modern world are to grow in the lives of individuals, as well as among any groups of individuals who may get together within or without the life of organized local churches. And if it also be asked when and how these laymen, or any groups of them, will grow in relation to the organized life of the Churches, the answer is that it depends very much on the Churches, but more of that later. If, alas, the existing Churches are not concerned enough to seek God's purpose in this situation and to try to meet it, no doubt God will in his wisdom lead these laymen into new insights and into any organized forms which their growing understanding of their ministry in and to society should take.

In the light of these beliefs about God and man and the ministry of laymen in and to the world, what special tasks will confront them today? Societies are very different whether they be capitalist, communist, or uncommitted, whether they be comparatively affluent or relatively poor. They are all changing rapidly, although not in precisely the same ways or at the same rate. There are, however, common features and trends, and it is possible to consider some of the salient tasks which they present to laymen in their ministry in and to society.

It will be assumed that laymen appreciate that Christians have no blue-print for Utopia. Jesus Christ as the meaning of full human life is an implication not an image; he is a dynamic not a design. But laymen, as the Bible insists, must have visions, and their visions will be of the Day of the Lord, the Kingdom of God, the heavenly City coming down out of heaven. Laymen will also realize that the ever-present task is to select, with their fellow men of good will, more immediate objectives in every sphere of life and to give the thought, time, effort, and resources, including money, to the achievement of those limited but necessary aims. This involves the understanding of, and the taking responsibility for, social institutions and associations whether they be large or small, powerful or weak. It means that some laymen will find themselves "in the corridors of power", that others will be administrators and executives, that others still will give professional services or scientific knowledge or technical skill, that others will undertake more ordinary tasks and should try to be informed and articulate citizens, workers, neighbours, and parents.

The world today is one world; but it is torn apart by the growth of nationalism and the divisions between the haves and the have nots.[7] Laymen have enormous tasks as politicians, administrators, and technical men, supported by ordinary citizens, to forge the international institutions needed to reduce strife and to build up one world which will be more just and equal.

New nation States, many of them avowedly secular and pluralistic, are coming into being and States which have some political maturity, some of which are still "Christian" in theory, are also confronted by enormous problems of social purpose and human well-being. New policies will involve the fashioning of political, financial, economic, educational, and all other social institutions as knowledge grows and technical skills increase. At every level of political decision and in every aspect of administration and citizenship the layman has his ministry in national society.[8]

Urbanization is now a world-wide phenomenon. For good or ill man wants to live in cities. Social scientists and theologians[9] are now able to show us that this is for good as well as ill, however it may look in a shanty town in the third world or a racial ghetto in the U.S.A., or a backward co-operative in a Communist society. Although national and international politics and economics may influence the life of cities it is in local politics and administration that many laymen can best make their presence felt. However difficult it may be there is opportunity at every level of citizenship even in the most repressive and restrictive forms of society. In societies in which there is political democracy laymen need encouragement to work with all men who will seek out reasonable objectives and pursue them. Such men will include planners, architects, and sociologists; so that ugliness, squalor, overcrowding, and all attendant evils may be tackled and the "milieu" for all the opportunities for good human living at work and at play may be made beautiful and appropriate.[10]

Industrialization is also coming in some fashion and degree to all countries. Can the newer countries reap the benefits and avoid some of the mistakes of earlier industrialization in the U.K. or the U.S.A., or in the U.S.S.R., or even in Japan? Only if large-scale industrial and commercial corporations, involving industrialists, managers, technical men, workers' leaders, and workers can learn fast and apply their knowledge to the increasing volume of new techniques and new skills. But industrialization is more than business organization, it interpenetrates every aspect of society, it separates classes, it divides homes from workplaces, it becomes the culture of the working community, it turns everyone into customers. Laymen in society and particularly in industry, in every role and function, have much to do today to refashion the whole understanding of industry as a profitable undertaking for the service of people. There are opportunities to work out anew standards of practice and the better organization of work by managers and technical men and workers. Industry has to be seen as a co-operative enterprise in which all participate to the best of their ability in the organization of the work to be done. It means a new look at the sharing of the tasks and the division of the rewards. All societies need a more balanced assessment of the relation of work to leisure and to rest.[11]

And lastly, one may consider the responsibilities of laymen in neighbourhoods and family life. Their *diakonia* or service has already been mentioned. In addition they have to perceive and pursue immediate objectives as they face the possibilities and problems of new community life. They must seek new ways of co-operation, in the family as well as in society, between the old and the young, between men and women, and between parents and children. All laymen must be involved in this task in and to society.[12]

Finally, it may be asked, what must the organized Churches do to encourage and support laymen in such ministry? There is only space to outline this briefly:

1. Many such laymen will demand that the Churches shall change their minds, that is, repent and be prepared to think again and to redeploy their resources to face the challenges of the modern world. They will want the organized Churches to seek unselfishly the good of society and not be so concerned with the selfish ends of any Church as an organization. Many laymen, and especially younger laymen, will want Churches to discern when to be responsible allies of powerful institutions and associations in society and when to challenge them in revolutionary ways in the name of God and man.

2. Some laymen will want church leaders especially to be concerned to stand by the leaders in society who are the decision-makers and opinion-formers, whether they would call themselves Christians or not, with sensitive understanding and relevant help in judgement about action.

3. Some laymen will want the organized Churches at every level not only to encourage all laymen to exercise their ministry in and to society according to their capabilities, responsibilities, and their selected priorities based on interests and opportunities, but also the local churches to understand and support such ministry in society by informed appreciation and by prayer. They will want local churches, if they want them at all, to be places in which they can obtain some respite from the world in meaningful worship, and in which, as a home-base, they can be re-educated and reinformed in order to be the salt of cleansing, the light of illumination, and the leaven of change in the world. They will not want the local church to be an ark of refuge, or a retreat, or even a community centre, or a sphere of stewardship. If it is a place in which they can think through their purposes, their priorities, their policies, and talk about them with other people of like commitment, many will gladly pay for what they believe in and then they can get on better with their stewardship in the world!

4. Not a few laymen in society will want the clergy to be well educated in a theology which is lively and meaningful to modern man in terms of contemporary knowledge and society. They will want to use him, if he is informed, articulate, and sensitive as a "resource man" to enable them to do better. He need not be a specialist in any social science or social skill, but he needs to know enough about the world in which he lives in general and to be glad to listen to laymen talking about the things they know about in particular. If that is so, they will want him to talk with them on the basis of his faith in God and man, his understanding of what this implies for human life, for judgement, decision, and action.

5. Many laymen will want the organized Churches at every level to plan new forms of church life and ministry, for example,

(*a*) Churches should appoint at national and diocesan level more clergy and laymen (as always including women in the word men) who have prepared themselves to educate others better in aspects of the ministry of laymen which have been described.[13]

(*b*) More lay institutes or centres for laymen are needed in which they can be better educated for their tasks in and to society. They need to have a secular flavour and a secular style. More is learned if such institutes are available to Christians and non-Christians together. In the dialogue faith and commitment, expert knowledge and skill, opportunities of, and problems for, judgement, decision, and action can be considered together. In such personal encounter all these features interact and enlighten. Such centres of education encourage and build up laymen and men of good will by increasing their knowledge, by helping them to be more articulate, and by stimulating their activity.[14]

(*c*) New initiatives in ministry by clergy and laymen are required, particularly at the local level. In these the clergy should be regarded as official representatives of the Church and as "resource men" and "enablers" of the laymen as, for instance, in some particular sphere, e.g. University or College Chaplains, Industrial Missioners, Ministers in cities and towns to councillors and administrators in national and/ or local government, to professional or commercial institutions, to various associations and groups. Deployment of clergy in such ministries might be associated with the organization of team or group ministries in urban and/or rural areas. The primary aim of all such new endeavours should be the encouragement and support of laymen in their ministry in and to society in the modern world.

Is it too bold to suggest that some such theological and social understanding of the ministry of laymen in and to society is the primary, if not the only, way in which God's care for the world and his Church and his purposes for the renewal of society and the Church will be advanced today?

NOTES

1. Yves Congar, O.P., *Lay People in the Church* (English Translation of *Jalons pour une théologie du laicat*). Geoffrey Chapman, 1957; Hendrik Kraemer, *A Theology of the Laity*. Lutterworth, 1958; S. Neill and Hans-Reudi Weber, *The Layman in Christian History*. S.C.M. Press 1963; Kathleen Bliss, *We The People*. S.C.M. Press paperback, 1963; Mark Gibbs and T. Ralph Morton, *God's Frozen People*. Fontana Books, 1964.
2. J. A. T. Robinson, *On Being the Church in the World*. S.C.M. Press, new edition 1963.

3. Kathleen Jones, *The Compassionate Society*. S.P.C.K., 1967.
4. Leonard Hodgson, *For Faith and Freedom*. Gifford Lectures, especially Vol. II. Blackwell, 1957.
5. David Jenkins, *The Glory of Man*. Bampton Lectures. S.C.M. Press, 1966.
6. John C. Bennet (ed.), *Christian Social Ethics in a Changing World*. Vol. I prepared for the W.C.C. Conference on Church and Society. Particularly the essay, "From Tribalism to Nationhood" by Adeolu Adegbola of Nigeria and the essays in Part V including one, "Conversion and Social Transformation" by Emilio Castro of Uruguay. S.C.M. Press, 1966.
7. Denys Munby (ed.), *Economic Growth in World Perspective*. Vol. III prepared for the W.C.C. Conference on Church and Society. Particularly the essay, "Issues for Christians" by Paul Abrecht, S.C.M. Press, 1966; Barbara Ward, *Space Ship Earth*. Hamish Hamilton, 1966.
8. Z. K. Matthews, (ed.), *Responsible Government in a Revolutionary Age*. Vol. II prepared for W.C.C. Conference on Church and Society. Particularly essays in Part V, "The Church and the Christian Citizen in Secular Society" by contributors from the U.S.A., Japan, the U.K., and Germany. S.C.M. Press, 1966; Egbert de Vries (ed.), *Man in Community*. Vol. IV prepared for the W.C.C. Conference on Church and Society. Particularly the essay, "Dynamics of a Pluralistic Society—the Indian Experience" by C. L. Itty. S.C.M. Press, 1963.
9. Harvey Cox, *The Secular City*. S.C.M. Press, 1965.
10. Edwin Barker (ed.), *The Responsible Church*. Essays prepared for the Social Responsibility Board of the Church of England. S.P.C.K., 1966.
11. J. H. Oldham, *Work in Modern Society* (this pamphlet is out of print but is still well worth searching for in a library). S.C.M. Press, 1950; Josef Pieper, *Leisure the Basis of Culture*. Faber & Faber, 1952.
12. *The Family in Contemporary Society*. Report prepared for the Lambeth Conference in 1958 (although dated, it contains material theological and social which is still useful). S.P.C.K., 1958.
13. Mollie Batten, Articles in *Theology*: "Theological Education" (Vol. LXVIII, No. 535, January 1965); "The Education of the Laos" (Vol. LXVIII, No. 540, June 1965).
14. *Centres of Renewal for Study and Lay Training*. An account of the Work of Academies and Lay Training Centres in Europe, North America, Asia, Africa, and Latin America. W.C.C., 1964.

3

Laymen in Ministry

JAMES MARK

This paper overlaps to some extent with those on Laymen in Mission and Laymen in Society; I assume that "ministry" means in this context those activities which have traditionally fallen to the ordained clergy, though perhaps with some measure of lay help: the conduct of worship, pastoral care, and theological thought. The third paper is presumably to refer to those activities of organized society which are normally carried on by laymen. Mission overlaps with ministry since both are concerned with the spreading of the faith; it overlaps with the activity of laymen in society since the mission may not be expressed in explicitly evangelistic terms, but implicitly through whatever the Christian does in that part of society with which he or she is concerned. We must recognize that the ministry of the laity has to do with everything that layfolk do. The distinctions which we make for the purposes of analysis and discussion are convenient but not fundamental.

This paper might have been written in a number of ways. It might survey the kinds of help which lay people give and go on to suggest ways in which that help might be extended. It might give the writer's own views about the place of the laity in the life of the parish—not an unpopular subject nowadays. I do not wish to do either of these things. I have no special competence for the first, and I assume that those who are to discuss the papers will possess greater and more varied collective knowledge of what is happening. Nor do I think that a statement of personal views, even if I wished to make it, would be the most helpful contribution to that discussion. I shall be concerned, rather, with questions prior to either kind of statement, on which the participants may wish to reflect before formulating their views: with the necessary prolegomena to the discussion, rather than with its practical details. The specific suggestions which I shall offer at the end of the paper are no more than tentative illustrations of the implications of what precedes them.

I assume at the outset that the laity should do as much as possible, and therefore that one should ask, not what they can usefully do to help, but what functions must be reserved to the clergy either for the present or, so far as one can see, permanently, either because they demand expertise which the laity cannot hope to command, or because the priest has the status which is required for their performance. I shall therefore be as much concerned with the functions of the clergy as with those of the laity. Conversely, are there ways in which the distinctive experience of laymen (one should perhaps use the plural) enable them to make distinctive contributions which the clergy cannot make unless they happen to have shared that experience? These questions of expertise and status go to the root of the matter. How expert are the clergy? In what does their separate status consist? In a short paper such as this I cannot hope to do more than throw out suggestions, assumptions, or dogmatic assertions on these matters, but what I say may at least serve as a starting-point for discussion. It must be said if useful discussion is to take place.

The distinctive experience of the clergy is, or should be, most evident in theology; and, since everything that a priest does is or should be derived from theological understanding in the broadest sense, it will be as well to refer to this first of all. One must distinguish between the pursuit of theology as a learned discipline and the contribution to the contemporary discussion of theological issues, on the one hand, and the theological understanding which should form the work of every priest, rather as one would distinguish between the work of a scholar in jurisprudence and that of a practising lawyer. Few priests are professional theologians, but all have some theological training; they therefore possess an expertise which few laymen can claim. All professions have their expertise, but the degree to which it separates the professional from the layman depends on two things: firstly on the degree of technicality of the professional knowledge, and, secondly, on the extent to which the subject impinges on life as we all live it, and on the interests which we all have in common. Few laymen can hope nowadays to contribute to the debate on progress in the natural sciences, though they may be able to comment on the general implications of this progress. Laymen cannot understand the more technical aspects of economic analysis, but they can say a good deal about the assumptions underlying the economist's thought. In literary

and artistic criticism the professional expertise is less easy to demon-
strate. The wide experience of the professional should count for a
great deal, but professionals are notoriously often less sensitive and
percipient than amateurs. Theology is in somewhat the same case.
The amateur cannot hope to possess the same degree of knowledge in
those parts of the field where it is decisive (for example, textual
criticism or church history), but religion, like the arts, is concerned
at close quarters with questions which concern most of us as human
beings: "Am I alone in the world or am I in the hand of God?"; "Is
this life all or what happens to me when I die?" "What relevance
have these questions to what I do with my life?" Moreover, when
theology gets beyond a very limited range of concrete questions, such
as those which arise in textual criticism, its subject-matter is the
vaguest and hardest to grasp of all, so that expertise in handling it
becomes very difficult to judge. Indeed, some contemporary philo-
sophers would argue that there can be none, since the questions at issue
are unreal ones, in that no answers can be offered. The professional
theologian may be better able than the layman to offer some kind of
answer to these questions if his professional knowledge is relevant and
if he has the necessary intellectual sensitivity, but there is no particular reason why the two should go together. We may have to content
ourselves with what the theologian can offer us within his specialized
field.

We need not discuss what contribution the layman can make to
theological writing and discussion, since no problem arises in the
present context. There is no procedure in the Anglican Church for
authorizing laymen to contribute, and they will no doubt show what
they can do. (The problem might arise in church government, when
what is at issue is the extent to which the laity should participate in
discussions of doctrine, but that is another matter.) The question is
rather what contribution laymen can make to those communal
activities of the Church for which theological knowledge and insight
are particularly necessary.

The conduct of worship is a function which, in the Anglican Communion, falls for the most part to the clergy (certainly in England)
and is always carried out under their authority and supervision. The
degree of expertise which it demands is not very great. The forms of
worship are, to a large extent, set and it is not difficult to learn how to
conduct them without falling into errors. There is, of course, need for
a great deal of skill and insight if they are to be appropriate to the

occasion and satisfying to the worshippers. This involves an understanding of the act of worship as a whole and in its separate parts,
and an ability to express and convey its intention. The person
responsible must have some appreciation of Anglican liturgical forms
and language, and also a degree of empathy with the congregation
and of insight and discrimination (which goes together with that
empathy) in the choice of occasional prayers. All this is very greatly
helped by the much wider experience of the priest and by his more
intimate knowledge of his congregation, which should enable him to
mould the form of worship, so far as he can, to meet their needs.
Nevertheless the *technical* expertise involved is relatively small; it
would not compare, for example, with that needed by a chartered
accountant examining a balance sheet. The less tangible qualities of
sympathy, insight, and discrimination may be possessed equally by
the layman. All that can be said is that since the priest has chosen this
particular vocation and has greater experience in this kind of function,
there is a presumption (but not, alas! a certainty) that he will possess
these to an unusual degree.

The field of pastoral care raises some complex differentiations.
First of all, one must distinguish between the different types of such
care. There seem to me to be four main ones: they have to do with
problems of belief and the devotional life; with the more general
problems which arise in personal and communal life (i.e. problems of
personal morality and social obligation); with problems which require
some kind of specialist advice (psychiatric, social, or even legal); and
with what an anthropologist would call the rites of passage—baptism,
confirmation, marriage, burial. Those which require specialist advice
fall for the most part outside the priest's field; unless he has special
training in the kind of problem involved, his function can only be to
seek the right kind of advice for his parishioner and to maintain a
general pastoral oversight, in so far as this is helpful. They fall equally
outside the field of the lay parishioner. The priest may be able to turn
to an individual parishioner who can supply the specialist advice, but
counselling of this kind is usually done professionally. Pastoral care
of the second kind does not require the specialist skills which the
priest may possess, though his background of theological understanding may help. Whether the person in need of help of this kind
can better get it from the priest or from a layman (and—what is more
important—to which he will turn) is a question of rapport; it will
depend, for example, on the position and standing of the priest in his

parish and on whether he is thought to have the sympathy and knowledge of life which will make it rewarding to consult him. The same is
true in a lesser degree of advice on questions of belief and devotional
life. Here the layman has traditionally looked to the priest; whether
he does so nowadays may well depend on whether or not he feels that
the priest is sensitive to the questions which laymen want to ask,
rather than to those which the priest may expect him to ask, and
which he has been prepared by his theological training to answer.
There may nowadays be a great difference between the two types of
question. Whether the man in need of advice of this kind will or can
turn profitably to another layman is another question.

The pastoral care connected with rites of passage is most clearly a
matter for the priest. We feel this instinctively, and it is instructive to
ask ourselves why. The answers which suggest themselves bring us to
the second factor to be considered in distinguishing between the functions of clergy and laity—that of the special status of the clergy. On
these occasions the priest is held to be in a special position. What he
has to do is not technically very difficult. The pastoral care which may
be needed certainly makes demands on his theological training, his
experience, and his sympathy. But the special status attributed to him
derives to a large extent from the belief that these are mysteries of
which he is the steward.

The priest in the Anglican Communion is certainly regarded as
someone set apart, having a special status (whether this is revered or
derided), and as the sole appropriate person (save in special cases of
emergency) to do certain things. Nor is this peculiar to the Anglican
Church (or, of course, in an even greater degree of the Roman
Church); it is nearly as true of the Free Churches in England. A
simple account of the reasons would be that the priest has received
the grace of orders; he has been set apart in accordance with dominical commandments, recorded in the New Testament and perhaps
supplemented by the experience of the Church (however defined) as
interpreted by the ecclesiastical authorities. These are the terms in
which the matter has traditionally been discussed; their characteristic
feature is that the appeal to Scripture or to the tradition of the
Church is held to give a special authority which would not be claimed
for other texts or arguments from history. But this kind of argument
notoriously runs into difficulties. Scripture is interpreted in different
ways; and different views are taken of the tradition of the Church and
what this establishes about the nature of the priesthood. Not all

these interpretations can be right. Secondly, the critic who does not choose to debate the matter in these terms may reflect that in no other intellectual discipline would such confident assertions be based on such slender evidence, whether it be the fragmentary and often ambiguous biblical texts or Church tradition. The earlier part of this is imperfectly known; and it is all too easy, in interpreting it, to choose and emphasize those facts which support one's own case, and to fail to take account of those factors which may have shaped that tradition and which may themselves have changed.

It seems wiser—especially in these ecumenical days—to base one's analysis of the peculiar nature of the priesthood more broadly on its derivation from religious experience and, in particular, on the relationships created by communal religious activities. That experience is certainly communicated to us through the New Testament and through the history of the Church, but in interpreting it we need to have regard to the limitations and imperfections of the media. We must not try to make the New Testament say more than it does. We must see the Church as the community of all believers, and have regard to the different forms of relationship between priesthood and laity which develop in different environments. In doing so we may find ourselves thinking less in terms of dogmatic assertion and more in terms of the sociology of different types of religious groups which have developed in different circumstances.

What does seem clear is that in all but small groups of certain kinds the priest or minister is the central figure and takes the lead. The emphasis varies, but even in Free Church congregations it does not appear that the layman attempts to put himself beside the minister. If the latter is present certain functions are reserved for him. Only in such types of congregation as the Friends' Meeting does it seem possible to dispense with the leadership of the ordained ministry. Certainly in the Church of England, whatever the talk in recent years of the ministry of the laity, it seems to me virtually impossible to imagine a situation in which the priest does not take the lead, except in small groups which may meet (for example, in factories or offices) for Bible study or discussion. We all know that if the priest is in some way inadequate or at odds with his congregation, the life of the congregation withers. I do not know of cases in which the lay members of the congregation have taken matters into their own hands and restored the position. We remain a priest-centred Church. The reasons for this are complex. First of all, the priest is in some sense the professional. Whatever his limitations he is nearly always better equipped for the job as a whole than any of his parishioners, even though some of them may possess knowledge and skills which enable them to do better than he some of the things the priest has traditionally done; and even though individual laymen may have a better grasp of the theological issues in which the congregation is interested. Moreover, in most cases he does, after all, devote his whole time to the job, whereas the layman can help only in his spare time. Thirdly, any group depends on leadership, and the priest, with these advantages, is best placed to supply it. Underlying all these more specific reasons is the feeling that he is, in some sense, steward of the mysteries, set apart from his fellow men. It seems overwhelmingly true that religious groups require someone of this type. Few men believe that Whitehead's statement that religion is what a man does with his solitariness is true, or at least that it is the whole truth. So long as their religious life finds expression in corporate activity, it seems that the priest will have his special role.

It is not surprising, therefore, that there are few signs of lay initiative. There is much talk nowadays of the need to enlarge the role of the laity, and to break down the traditional relationships between clergy and laity. There is just as much talk of the need for new forms of organization and worship to supplement, if not to replace, the parochial structure and the forms of worship associated with it. The discussion seems to be confined to a small minority—much smaller among the laity than among the clergy. Changes are probably desirable, but it would be mistaken to think that there is widespread or intense pressure among the laity for them. There may be a good deal of diffused and not very clearly formulated feeling that the present situation and the present ways of doing this are unsatisfactory, but this may be stronger among those who do not come to church than among those who do.

What I have said implies that any worth-while attempt to redefine the functions of the laity in the ministry of the Church involves thinking out afresh the place of the visible Church in the life of the world. It is perfectly possible to avoid this, to limit oneself to suggesting new types of job which the laity might undertake in order to devote some of their increasing leisure to helping out the hard-pressed clergy, but this would hardly tackle the problem seriously. One has to ask such questions as whether or not the structure of church life and the forms of worship need to be changed, and if so how; to what extent, in an age when the traditional language and thought-forms of theology have to be looked at afresh, the clergy should lean more on the experience of the layman in seeing the problems with which theology needs to be concerned? The paradox is that very few of the laity see these problems clearly, though far more may have some more or less unformulated consciousness that they exist. A peculiar responsibility rests upon the clergy in this situation. They have to encourage the laity to recognize the problems and to consider how their responsibilities may be changing. This is not easy. Professional groups of any kind find it hard to review their own status and functions with an unprejudiced eye; the difficulties are likely to be greater when their preconceptions are thought to be backed by theological authority. It may be argued that, unless and until the laity show more sign of concern about these matters, there is no point in the clergy trying to stimulate such a concern. The answer is surely that it is for those who can see to point out what should concern us all. This is not to say that the clergy should do their thinking in isolation from the laity. There must be a dialogue, though for the most part the clergy must start it. And the starting-point should be frank discussion of what the laity feel that they need of the visible Church (both those who take part in its worship and those who do not); what questions they wish to ask and what contribution they can make from their own knowledge and experience.

In England, at least, the Church of England being what it is, things are not likely to change rapidly. They will change most slowly, if at all, in those matters which have been thought of traditionally as the peculiar preserve of the clergy: the administration of the sacraments, the occasional offices and the pastoral care associated with them, or questions of devotional life. Outside these activities a good deal might change with advantage, so long as we look for a lay contribution which is distinctive rather than supplementary. Lay readers play a very necessary part, but we need to give more opportunity in the pulpit to laymen who have the necessary theological insight to be able to speak from their experience of the world and who will speak not merely as substitutes for the clergy. They can bring their experience to bear, similarly, in the discussion of questions of faith and morals, and in a great deal of pastoral activity which they might undertake.

The point of this paper, however, is not to make a list of new activities for the layman. We shall be more likely to develop the right forms of activity if we begin by asking the right questions. I have tried to suggest what these should be.

4

Priesthood

LESLIE HOULDEN

This paper does not aim to give a comprehensive account of the theological issues included in its subject, nor does it attempt a neutral dispassionate survey of those topics which have been selected for treatment. Rather, by taking its own positive way and departing from customary idiom, it seeks to stimulate and forward discussion of priesthood.

We must begin by defining our subject, for the term priesthood is not free from ambiguities. It may refer simply to the second order of ministry in the traditional scheme, those clergy who are neither bishops nor deacons. Here we wish to use it more generally than that, to denote the normal, central exercise of ministry in the Church, wherever it is found and in whatever way it is arranged. Some will prefer not to use this word for this purpose, and we shall attempt to meet some of their objections (though sometimes obliquely) in the course of this essay. In using the word as widely as this, we include, alongside those who technically bear the name of priests, all (such as bishops and non-episcopal ministers) who carry out that amalgam of worshipping, preaching, teaching, and caring which makes up the normal work of the Christian clergy. The fact that there are some in holy orders whose work does not chiefly fall under these headings at first sight creates an anomaly: to them we shall return in due course. We start from what remains the normal area of activity of the vast majority of Christian clergy.

But the term priesthood is not the only one to yield this area of meaning. Ministry or clergy would do almost as well for precisely the same purpose, though neither of them is easily confined to those we have in mind. But priesthood is our subject, and if we are to use it in the general sense just suggested, we must note its special flavour and associations. At the outset, discussion is bedevilled by a mistake and a confusion, both of them responsible for theological difficulty which is at least partly unnecessary.

We look first at the mistake, which results from a piece of imperfect typology. In the early Church, and in the church in North Africa particularly, one way of relating the Old Covenant to the New was by way of a simple parallelism of ingredients. The arrangements and institutions of the old religion of Israel demonstrated what was, so to speak, the right equipment which authentic religion ought to possess; the arrangements of the Church could be expected to display the same features, albeit in a new form. Thus, baptism corresponded to circumcision, Sunday to Sabbath, Eucharist to the old sacrifices, and Christian priesthood to Aaronic. Clearly, such a procedure may be edifying and instructive, but it can also lead into dangerous paths when used as a basis for theology. Above all, the role of Christ in this pattern is too incidental. As far as the actual structure of the pattern is concerned, he is simply the agent who ends the old regime and begins the new; but he is hardly the key point in any more organic sense than this.

In true typology, on the other hand, Christ is the control; by reference to his life, death, and resurrection alone can it be determined which Old Testament themes and images are appropriate to illuminate him and which are to emerge for transformed service in the thought and language of the Church. The old images all come to meet in him; the new all spring from him. The unsuitable ones are discarded, and none has any validity which is independent of him.

Much of the unease at the term priesthood comes from its use in theological statement which belongs to imperfect typology. This is at work when the priest is seen as the one whose chief task (the one that gives him this title) is to offer the Eucharist, the sacrifice of the New Covenant, just as Aaronic priests offered the sacrifices of the Old. Such statement may or may not be appropriate, but whether it is or not depends solely upon its coherence with true typology (that is, valid use of the term priesthood to describe the clergy must be derived from the theology of the person and work of Christ and not on a pattern based on mere parallelism, however neat and attractive). So much for the mistake.

The confusion results from over-devotion to the letter of New Testament texts as raw materials for theological statement. It is true that in the New Testament the term priest is hardly applied to anyone who could conceivably be thought of as a clergyman (the nearest is St Paul in a fleeting metaphor in Romans 15.16 and Philippians 2.17). It is applied to Christ (Heb. 5.1–10; 8.1f; John 17). It is applied perhaps to God (Rom. 3.25), and certainly to the Christian people, both in the present (1 Pet. 2.5–9) and in the future (Rev. 5.10; 20.6). The temptation is to suppose first that Christians ought never to use the term except in one of these senses, and secondly that these varied uses ought somehow to be capable of being related to one another *in terms of the word priest*.[1] In truth there is no problem here, at least not in this form. It is a matter of the same image or concept being used by independent writers in a variety of ways for a number of different purposes for which it seemed to them appropriate. This is a perfectly understandable procedure which contans no mystery and does not call for the harmonizing of the different applications. Nor does it carry with it a demand that the term should not be applied to the clergy if the image is in some way appropriate to describe their function. To apply it to the clergy in this way implies no disparagement of the Christian people as a whole: it can be applied to them to make equally valid but different points. It is a matter of defining the precise function of the image in each particular case. Certainly, when the writer of 1 Peter applies the term to the whole Christian people, he is not attributing some sort of clerical status to all Christians in any modern sense, nor is he affirming that clerical office is to be excluded or lightly esteemed by Christian theology; he is not raising issues of this kind at all. Similarly, when the work of Christ is described in priestly terms in the Epistle to the Hebrews, nothing is being either affirmed or denied about Christian clergy; the matter is not in mind. The most that can be said is that the uses of this image of priesthood in the New Testament may contribute to the building up of a theological framework which excludes certain views of the status and role of the clergy; but this is nothing to do with the term priest itself—it is a matter of a whole pattern of doctrine.

Though the mistake and the confusion to which we have referred have caused much gratuitous difficulty in discussion of this matter, real issues lie behind them—often less to do with priesthood itself than with other, more central doctrinal matters such as the work of Christ and the believer's relationship with him. As we turn now to make a constructive statement of the theology of priesthood, these matters will be continually in mind, and we shall endeavour to do them justice as far as the scope of the discussion permits.

We must state our principles. First, nothing whatsoever impairs the uniqueness of Christ as the bearer of God to man and as the means of man's return to God. The uniqueness consists in the totality of his giving of himself to the Father for these ends, and in the divine place which he occupies in God's action towards man for their accomplishment. It clearly does not imply that others do not also perform these tasks *in their own proper manner and degree*. Holy men of all kinds, whether Christian or not, participate in the work of bearing God to man and enabling man to return to God. We therefore relate the activity of these men to that of Christ by speaking of it as a participation in his unique mediatorial role. Whether they do it consciously or not, all such men share in the divine purpose which Christ embodies, but they do it wholly by dependence upon him. By baptism all Christians are potentially of this company because they are in the sphere where the articulate word of the gospel is heard, and so can bring to bear upon others the work of Christ with all fullness and clarity. Whatever is to be said about the clergy's particular role, it must be consistent with this.

Secondly, nothing whatever impairs the equality of all Christians in their direct relationship with God and in their enjoyment of the benefits of Christ's work. But equality in these crucial respects leaves .entirely open the possibility of inequality in other respects, and makes it neither more nor less likely that such inequality is consistent with God's purposes. It is clear, for example, that several New Testament writers were far from extending the equality of all Christians to the exercise of functions in the Church. St Paul welcomed the fact that a wide variety of charismata was bestowed upon the members of a relatively small congregation (1 Cor. 12), and saw in this nothing incompatible with their equal participation in the Christian status. Whether a particular Christian group puts more stress on the respects in which Christians are equal or the respects in which they are unequal depends commonly upon factors which are only loosely related to Christian theology. Thus, excessively rigid hierarchy or the disesteeming of some parts of the Christian community and the exalting of others (usually the laity and the clergy respectively!) result from political, economic, and social pressures which are not difficult to identify. In such circumstances, theological argument tends to limp behind the situation it must somehow justify. Similarly, the strong and overriding assertion of the equality of all Christians is often more a reaction against over-rigid hierarchy than a really valid generalization from those respects in which it is undoubtedly justified.

The third principle is connected with the fact that differentiation of function within the Christian community does not in itself impair Christian equality, and leads us to the reason why this is so. We propose to give full value to the fact that God's work is thoroughly sacramental in character. With Christ himself as the supreme instance, God communicates himself to man through people, things, and acts. Even abstract ideas are always indissoluble from the personalities and circumstances of those who formulate and utter them. The word is always made flesh. The people, things, and acts which are God's sacramental agents come to man intimately, intensively, and radically, if he allows them to do so, and affect his whole person and life. Those rites which the Church names technically as sacraments are of course central examples of this. Too often, because they seem small in their effects by comparison with the great power inherent in them, they are expounded in terms other than these. Either they are made to depend for their reality upon human response, and so their standing as acts of God is neglected, or they are accorded a rather harsh, impersonal objectivity in the attempt to make them as independent as possible of the response given to them. But God's action is nothing if not personal in its character; what he proffers to man, in sacraments as in all his other actions, is his whole self, seeking union with each human creature. His action always, then, aims at the most profound effects upon man and means to achieve them in the end. It goes without saying that the personal character of God's action means that it is never a matter of generality but always of particularity. It is the same Eucharist which feeds all God's people, but what God designs to accomplish by it in the life of each is entirely moulded to the needs of each. It follows that in a world created and indwelt by God it is important never to undervalue theologically, never to minimize divine significance in rites and institutions where it ought to be maximized. Wherever God acts, he acts fully.

Priesthood is to be understood in the light of these considerations. This is so first in relation to the functions which the clergy perform in the setting of the whole Church. Continually, they act as sacramental persons, instruments of God's purposes in a wide variety of ways. However "low" a doctrine of the ministry a Christian group may have, it cannot prevent such officers as it possesses acquiring a representative character, and this inevitably shapes the character of their work. They act not only in their individual capacities, with their personal talents and defects, but as standing for God in the Christian community. To that degree and in that sense their action always has an impersonal aspect. But in the sense that it is always the action of one man towards others, their work is always intensely personal— and so the appropriate means of God's personal action towards us. Of course, on this second side, the bearer of priesthood cannot be distinguished in certain ways from any other Christian; but his representative capacity does give him a special place. We must not accord this a merely incidental significance; the differences of function within the Church are themselves means of grace (charismata) and not just convenient ways of getting some of the Church's work done (that is, they convey to the Christian community, in visible personal form, various facets of the divine work and character). This is the proper function of hierarchy in the Church, and as long as it acts in this way, it does nothing to spoil but rather enhances the essential equalities of the whole Christian people. When it fails to act thus, the results can of course be disastrous in that the structure of the Church's leadership turns out to belie the gospel it preaches. Thus a tyrant-bishop may well give to his subordinates many unsought opportunities for spiritual advancement through mortification of their wills, but he hardly serves to stimulate life-giving charity among his people.

The sacramental character of God's work points the way not only to the understanding of the work of priesthood, but also to the evaluation of those who bear it. In the first place, it explains why the name of priest should be a suitable one for the Christian clergy, why (to revert to our earlier remarks) this image should be appropriately applied in Christian usage to a body of men for whom the New Testament did not use it and to whom it was originally applied by a piece of imperfect typologizing. The image or idea of priesthood, especially in the biblical tradition, brings together a number of concepts: in particular, representation, mediation, sacrifice, and leadership of others into access to God. All these ideas apply in one way or another to the actual role of the Christian clergy. As we have seen, in whatever Christian group they exist, their representative function is inescapable, however strenuously the doctrinal implications of it are restricted. Inevitably too, the clergy's work involves acting as agents for transmitting the things of God to men, in particular the gospel and the sacraments, but also the pastoral care which the Church exercises as the instrument of the Good Shepherd. There is room for difference of opinion how far these tasks, undeniably associated with the clergy, should be confined to them. Some tasks, such as the pastoral, are not necessarily theirs alone, and it is worth asking whether there is any substantial theological reason why others (such as presiding at the Eucharist) should not similarly be regarded as only conventionally their sole province. To answer this, let us look more closely at the instance we have mentioned, the pastoral office. While no one would claim that this should be confined to the clergy, for it is clearly one aspect of the charity required of all Christians, it remains true that in actual fact it is most intensively exercised over the whole range of the Christian community by the clergy alone. Where others share in it, it is usually with regard to a few specific individuals (family or friends), or, in the case of those whose profession is pastoral in nature (for example, teachers or nurses) with regard to one single category of persons (the young or the sick). In practice, then, the pastoral task is normally carried out, in the setting of the entire Christian community, by the clergy. And in a world sacramentally worked upon by God practice is far from incidental to theological statement. The practice is part of the empirical base for the action of God through priesthood and therefore for its theological significance in the whole work of God towards man.

The sacrificial associations of priesthood are equally important in that the clergy are called upon to bear the marks of that self-giving love which Christ shows to be the overriding characteristic of God. Again, this is something they share with all Christians, but still they exercise this role with special prominence. Once more, the practicalities are to be used theologically, for it is certainly the case that the sacrificial self-giving of the clergy, in prayer and in virtue, is the stimulus and encouragement from which others profit, and its lack is a scandal which frustrates the rest. In this respect as in others, the bearer of priesthood is the sacramental agent of God's own love centrally embodied in Christ.

Priesthood is associated with the leading of others into closer access to God. This was the aspect of priesthood upon which the author of Hebrews seized when he applied the image to the work of Christ. In their own different way, in strict dependence upon Christ and their life in him, the clergy share this characteristic. In their case it depends partly on their performance of certain acts where their personalities count little (baptizing, reading services), partly on their holiness of life, and partly on their technical expertise. Not all these features will be present in all clergy in substantial degree, but certainly they all belong to the function of priesthood. The last of the three is worth special note because it is often treated as if it were incidental to the essence of the matter. If it is left out of account, it becomes easier to treat the work of priesthood as a series of tasks, some apparently requiring little skill, which are allocated to certain persons in the Church by way of sheer convenience or order. This tendency in much modern discussion sees ordination as no more than an authorization by the Church, which forms, so to speak, only an outer skin upon its bearer. We shall see other reasons for being unwilling to accept this view, but one reason is certainly the existence of the technical skills, going to the roots of a man's being and attitudes, which the priest needs to possess. These are not simply the skills which a lay theologian equally possesses (for example, in biblical study, doctrine, or church history), but arise from the theological formation demanded by the specific work of priesthood. They are stimulated by, and directed towards, that work, and therefore include (for example) extra attention to ascetic and moral theology. Moreover all theology will be studied in the context of the needs of the work and so will have a pastoral and apologetic slant. The technical skills which the priest acquires over the years by a mixture of study and experience are another part of the data through which God uses these persons sacramentally, to be the agents of his work. Their theological significance is, in the world of a God who acts sacramentally, indissolubly bound up with their actual work and activity.

The sacramental approach to God's work also helps to evaluate the theological significance of priesthood, in that it draws attention to the extent of the divine action within the priest himself. God forms a man in his whole personality for perfect relationship with himself, and in so doing deals with him in his whole setting in life. The work which a man undertakes and the skills which he acquires are a most important part of that setting, and, far from being a superficial layer on top of his "real personality" are wholly integrated with him. It is a question of the relation of function to person. Christianly speaking, we are, presumably, never happy with a total divorce between the two though for certain purposes we are ready to tolerate it. When we have to buy groceries, we bear with the fact that the grocer is uncharitable or adulterous provided that he manages his business efficiently; pastorally speaking, in relation to him as a whole person, we are concerned to remedy the situation. In the case of a Christian, we desire that moral conduct should match the performance of outward Christian duties, and we look for such an integrity of person that it is meaningless to ask when he is acting as a Christian and when he is being himself.

In the case of the priesthood, nobody wants totally to divorce function from person, though some lines of discussion come perilously near it; quite often there is found an unwillingness to admit that anything is demanded of a clergyman, apart from function, that is not demanded equally of any other Christian. This undervalues the importance of function in relation to personality. Because the function differs, the demand also differs. The priest is to be a priest, whole and integrated, not a layman doing priestly tasks. The priesthood is to take hold of his whole personality, so that he lives what he is. It should be meaningless to ask of any of his significant thoughts or actions whether he is acting as a priest or as himself. The traditional notion of indelible character, juridical though it may be in some formulations (necessary perhaps to deal with hard cases), may usefully be considered along these lines. If a man becomes *this* kind of man with integrity, he cannot cease to be what he is.

Of course the same may be true of a Christian teacher or a Christian bricklayer. Only for certain purposes (the professional or the liturgical) is the division simply into clergy and laity, as the two categories comprising the Church, the meaningful one. For many purposes, we need to make many more divisions, as St Paul did. The Christian teacher will acquire one kind of integrated Christian being, resulting from the operation of grace upon his own personality and the needs of his calling, and the Christian bricklayer another. Yet nobody has ever claimed to ordain a man for life to Christian bricklayership, though if one may interpret the Pauline lists so, it may be that they once did see people as ordained to Christian teacherhood, and when a nun is professed in a teaching order, it is not much different from it. We do, however, make much more of ordaining clergy to permanent status; and this is wholly justifiable within the context of the Church as the microcosmic, pioneer community with mankind. For while the Church could survive (and almost does!) without Christian bricklayers and even without Christian teachers, it could not reasonably survive without priests. These particular people whose functions are indissoluble from their personality are essential to the Church: not just juridically, in that it has been laid down, for example, that the

Eucharist can be celebrated only by a bishop or a priest, but much more fundamentally, in that God can only mediate himself to man by means of other men, and the Church needs to externalize and focus certain necessary functions upon particular persons. Some of them can be done by others fragmentarily (for example, the pastoral function), but they need to find focal and central expression in those who will *be*, exist as, pastors (or whatever function one has in mind). Walking men need walking sacraments. As in marriage a man in relation to his wife experiences, and does not just think about, the love of Christ and his Church, so in relation to the priest a man experiences, and does not just think about, the divine fatherhood or the divine forgiveness; and this is appropriate to our human condition. Such a provision is of a piece with the nature of a Creator God and a God who incarnates himself within his creation.

This approach to the theology of priesthood has been concerned chiefly with the place of the clergy in the Church, but the same considerations can easily be extended to their work as representatives of Christ and his Church to those outside. Here again, the priest acts on behalf of Christ expressed in the Christian community, bearing his charity or the explicit word of the Gospel, as appropriate to the needs of those with whom he deals. In no case does he act as a solitary, simply on his own private credentials, but always as a sacrament of him whom he serves.

Because we have concentrated on the place of the clergy in the Church, we have also neglected all exercises of priesthood apart from the most central and normal: the priest in relation to a fairly static Christian group. There have long been many (priest-monks, school-masters in holy orders) who have been " off-centre " from this point of view. It is likely that at least in highly mobile Western society their number and variety will increase; the priest-worker, the chaplain to a single social group, the priest-religious—these are likely to be more and more in demand as agents of pastoral care and evangelism, or simply of Christian presence. But just as bad or unskilled priests do not affect the fact that the norm is a virtuous and competent priest, so such ways of exercising priesthood do not affect the fact that the normal place for the priest, theologically and in practice, is at the heart of the Christian community, which has the Eucharist for its typical manifestation of itself. This is where, as a sacramental person, he chiefly belongs; and the test of whether men acting outside this setting should be ordained or not will lie in the degree to which their roles seem to be reasonable deviations from the norm and retain enough of its features.

Because the priest is a sacramental person whose whole being is to be penetrated by God for the purposes of his calling, his ordinary humanity may seem in danger of being obliterated, as if ordination brought him into a caste apart. But this is not so, except in the sense that the particularity of each man makes him in God's eyes a caste of one! Rather, a man's ordinary humanity is enhanced by his discovering the role in which he is to grow towards God, and the priesthood is no exception. Renunciations which the priest may be called upon to make (for example, marriage or wealth, in certain cases) are no monopoly of his among the servants of God.

There are many other questions concerning priesthood, some of great importance, to which we have not even referred; but the approach we have adopted may point to a line of treatment for some of them. We have spoken of the thorough involvement of God in the rites and institutions which he gives to us and of maximizing their theological value (that is, seeing them fully as his acts). It seems to be consistent with this that the historical continuity of priesthood is a factor of importance, though only one element among others in assessing its value. How exactly it should be related to particular historical manifestations of priesthood is outside our scope. Whether it is consistent with this approach that women should be ordained is another topic which we do not propose to discuss, but certainly the question ought to be tackled in these terms. The psychological and social practicalities involved are not to be seen as factors which prevent clear abstract theology having free course, but are part of the data for making the theology.

It is often disputed whether the ministry is theologically prior to the Church or dependent upon it, whether its authority is from above or from below. It ought be to be clear that we should refuse to choose between such falsely posed alternatives. The Church simply exists, by God's disposition, in differentiated form: there are many gifts but one Spirit. Of course, therefore, the authority of the clergy to perform their functions is divinely conferred; but equally clearly this authority is exercised within the whole company of those who participate in Christ.

We have tried to confine ourselves to ways of speaking about priesthood which are true of it "in itself", and so to distinguish it from the various sociological roles which it is called upon to play. At a time when, in many parts of the world, these roles shift rapidly and men find it hard to adjust, it is all the more important to hold the essentials clearly and distinctly. We have also confined ourselves to discussion of priesthood in the general sense which we began by outlining. This office is amply held by the bishops and priests of Catholic Christendom, though in them and in all others it is impaired by the disunity of Christians, which prevents its bearers from acting unhaltingly as the sacraments of God's perfect charity. We have deliberately refrained from using the term to refer to the second of the three traditional orders of ministry and from discussing the issues raised by that narrower application. Priesthood is essentially a function (or a group of functions) which many different kinds of Christian clergy exercise, including many who are (with considerable justification, given the muddles which Christian usage has provided for it) reluctant to use the word to describe it.

It may seem that at a time when even the case for the worthwhileness of religious inquiry has often to shout loud for a hearing, the doctrine of priesthood is only of the most peripheral importance. But Christian faith is never happily divorced from Christian life, and it is hard in practice to have much experience of the Christian religion without being confronted with the Christian ministry. It may be important for a man to know how to think of it quite early in his contact with Christianity. He may need to know, for example, what kind of authority the clergyman carries. A man may even meet the priest before he knowingly meets God at all, and if at that stage he cannot be expected to understand the priest's significance, at least the priest himself ought to know whether his priesthood signifies much or little, and precisely what.

NOTE

1. So much so that there is sometimes a sense of mystification when this proves difficult. See, for example, *Conversations between the Church of England and the Methodist Church: A Report* (1963), p. 23: "A measure of theological uncertainty or disagreement as to the intrinsic nature of the priesthood of ordained ministers and its relation to the priesthood of the laity or of the whole Church is not intolerable, and is not incompatible with the establishment of communion between our two Churches or with fellowship in one Church."

5

Voluntary and Part-time Ministries

ERIC JAMES

"Gentlemen, I have news for you!" I said to the three dozen or so theological students I had asked to address at their theological college somewhere in England. "All your bishops have agreed to ordain you." The students, as I had hoped, were faintly amused and considerably sceptical. "Their lordships lay down only one condition", I continued. "Those of you who were earning your living before you came here must return to your jobs. You are, I imagine, quite willing for that." The young men smiled. They were clearly *not* willing. "But it is *ordination* you have been asking for and *ordination* you are getting", I insisted. The young men looked a little troubled. "Could it then be that you are not really wanting to be priests in the Church of God?—that really you are after a certain job-structure, not 'ordination'?" There was an uneasy silence. "What in fact are you after in asking for 'ordination'?" I asked. "Let's discuss that." So we did. We had to.

The young men were not greatly to be blamed. Ordination had for them an obvious sociological meaning as the rite of admission into a professional body with a loosely defined job-structure. But they had presumed they were giving it primarily a theological meaning. Only when the sociological setting was changed was the weakness of their purely theological conviction exposed.

It is probably the same for most clergy and laity. All sorts of new questions arise once the sociological setting of ordained ministry is changed, and is *seen* to have changed. Until that happens the theology of ordination is presumed to involve professional and full-time ministry. In the incident I have described some didactic violence was required to make the point and to gain openness to the fundamental questions. If such violence is required with young ordinands at a university, how much more violence may be required with those who have more reason to take the *status quo* for granted before real openness to new patterns of ministry is achieved!

Such openness certainly requires a full discussion of "what we are after in ordination". We shall not discuss this fully in this essay (there is another sub-committee and therefore another essay dealing directly with "the priesthood", and another with "the diaconate"), but it *must* be discussed, for otherwise recruitment, selection, and training for the ministry will all have after them the fundamental but unanswered question: "What for?"

Professor Douglas Webster reminds us that in the New Testament ministers are described primarily as ministers of God, ministers of Christ, and ministers of the gospel. Inevitably therefore in such a discussion we shall be involved not only in the Debate about the Shape of the Ministry, but in the Debate about God, and the Debate about Christ, and the Debate about the Gospel. Even when we have opted merely to discuss "voluntary and part-time ministries" we are in the thick of "The Christian Understanding of Revelation"; "Jesus Christ and Mythology"; "What is Secularization?", and so on. The Debate about the Shape of the Ministry must never be an escape from "the big questions"; it must always be carried on with "the big questions" not far from the front of the mind.

Openness to new patterns of ministry, to new meaning for ordination, to "the big questions"—openness is all. As Bishop Lesslie Newbigin has written in his preface to *New Forms of Ministry*:

> The question is not, "What special and exceptional arrangements must we make in order to keep the traditional pattern of the ministry from breaking under the new strains?" The question is, "What, in the new circumstances into which God has thrust us, is the pattern of the ministry which is proper to the nature of the Church as God's apostolic community in this world?"

Openness to this question has already forced many an ordained man to look again at the biblical picture of the shape of the ministry, where he has discovered with relief that the New Testament characteristically speaks of "varieties of ministry"; that our inherited conception of ministry is much more settled, inflexible, invariable than any pattern revealed in the New Testament. The New Testament certainly permits a minister to work as a professional, receiving his salary from the Church with a good conscience, but it also permits a minister for evangelical reasons to take an occupation which is *not* paid by the

Church, in order to continue to serve a specific community which cannot or will not support him. But someone today looking again at the biblical picture of the shape of the ministry is unlikely to look to it to provide a *detailed* shape of the ministry. He would not now expect to find the security of an invariable and unchangeable order of ordained ministry, laid down once and for all, in the pages of the New Testament and in the early Church. He will be glad to note what has seldom been noted in the past—the difference of function, the difference of situation, the variety, fluidity, openness to change, the absence of an invariable pattern of hierarchy, but he will not expect to find justification in the New Testament for the *details* of the shape of the ministry to the twentieth-century world. He is more likely to concede—as part of his openness and as part of his biblical theology of the world—that the world must to a considerable extent dictate the shape of the ministry. "The World is the Agenda." The Church has to speak to that agenda, and therefore its ordained ministry must be of such a shape as to be able to speak to it most effectively.

Openness to the world as it is can hardly fail to result in new patterns of ordained ministry. In the world that was, the static society, a locality was like a cartwheel. The rim of the wheel was the evident limit of the natural locality. The Church was at the hub of things. The community was small enough for the pastor to know his own and for his own to know him. He could call his own sheep by name. In many localities pastors were in plentiful supply—enough for a pastor to every locality—and the "establishment" situation provided enough money to keep this shape of the ministry going. But now the "cartwheel" is in urban society rarely an evidently separate locality (though the parochial system may assume it is). It has been submerged in the agglomeration, the conurbation. The "cartwheel" has become a series of cogwheels, for whereas people lived, learned, laboured, and spent their leisure within the "cartwheel", now they may live in one locality, learn in another, labour in another. The place of residence may be what Berthold Brecht has called the "vertical receptacle", the large unit of accommodation itself the size of a village (and if the church building is five hundred yards away from the "receptacle" it might as well be five hundred miles away. It is no longer within the locality). Education increasingly takes place in large units, another "cog-wheel". The size of industrial units increases. Leisure may be spent in the residential locality, but often in front of the T.V., being introduced to different localities around the globe—

without commitment—and thus not having "the locals" in or going out to "the local". Alternatively, there is the journey out of the locality in the car. We have to minister now more and more to an urban, mobile, plural, secular society, and we need "varieties of ministry", a plural ministry, for the task. To make any mark upon such a society a ministry more numerous than the full-time professional ministry now is required, so numerous that it is unlikely that in most situations it can be paid for by the Church. But even if the money were available, it is doubtful whether in a secular society the Church can serve and penetrate that society unless at least part of its ordained ministry earns its own living, gaining entrance to, and contact with, society by undertaking secular occupations.

And if voluntary and part-time ministries are now theologically and pastorally desirable in the mobile urban society, no less are they right and necessary in the rural situations. It is impossible to imagine many rural situations in which the Church will now be able to provide each small community with its own professional and full-time minister.

But if openness to the sociological realities of our present society may lead to new patterns of ordained ministry, it is important to recognize that our eyes have been closed (the social situation has been facing us for a century and more in some places) as much for theological reasons in the past—because, for instance, of our theology of the sacred and the secular. Only thirty-five years ago, Bishop Winnington-Ingram, then Bishop of London, in a Convocation debate, said, concerning the administration of the chalice by responsible laymen, that "the laity did not want to see somebody in that position on Sunday when they were going to do business with him on Monday". Clearly the Bishop believed that the administration of the sacrament was something that the holy man had better keep to himself and to Sunday and to the holy place. (The layman could *receive* Communion on Sunday: apparently that did not have any compromising effect upon him on Monday at his place of business!) And the Bishop was undoubtedly right to say "the laity do not want to see . . ."; for all too often the laity have been given a sub-Christian, even an anti-Christian understanding of holiness, in which the holy man, and the holy place, and the holy day are not separated in order that *all* men, *all* places, *all* days should be holy, but are merely separated, and a world of holiness is established over against the everyday world.

It would, nevertheless, be foolish to minimize the problem of the sacred and the secular—not least as it affects voluntary and part-time ministries. Are there any employments that can be judged inimical to ordained ministry? Is there *any*thing to be said for Cardinal Manning's dictum (quoted recently at the ordination in a South African diocese of the first men to be ordained to a "tent-making" ministry): "A blot upon a layman's coat is little seen; a spot upon an alb cannot be hid"? Any job which needs to be done is a Christian job, and therefore can be done by a minister of Christ; but undeniably there are some employments that are more congenial to ordained ministry than others.

Inevitably, when the possibility of voluntary and part-time ministry is envisaged, the rigid distinction between clergy and laity is called in question. In the recent and not so recent past clergy were almost all full-time; they came usually to the local church from outside; they were clearly a separate profession. "Vocation to the Ministry" has been thought of primarily as a subjectively experienced call to this profession. "I think I am being called to be a priest." Now it is important, surely, to recognize that this is quite different from the New Testament picture. In the New Testament there is an itinerant ministry, and, as we have said, some will have received their salary from the Church. But the local church could never have regarded those who came to them temporarily from outside as "*the* Ministry". There seems to have been frequent contact with apostolic direction by the comings and goings of St Paul and his colleagues in the itinerant ministry; but there is a local church which has elected its own ministry from within. And though there is little to suggest that churches merely stood by themselves, yet the reality and strength of the churches, and their power to "stand on their own feet" is notable. Certainly the call to ordained ministry is not primarily a subjective experience: in the main, men were called to ministry by the local church, to "varieties of ministry".

At the present time Christian Stewardship and the rediscovery of the importance and the role of the laity and of "laity training" is gradually meaning that every member of a congregation is being asked to consider how he can best serve Christ and his Church. People in many places are being asked to take on this and that work which needs to be done in the name of Christ. As a result many are willing to take on responsibilities which they would never have thought of accepting before. But there is still a great gulf fixed between this kind of attitude and the recognition that *every member of the Church ought to be trained for ministry, and that every local church ought in some way to be supplying the ordained ministry.* It is one thing to be doing this and that because "the Vicar asked me"—or even to see what one is doing and being asked to do as part of ministry in general. It is quite another for each local church to know itself deeply responsible for recruiting and supplying part of the commissioned and empowered ministry and for there to be organic and objective ways of calling such a ministry into being.

At this point it might be profitable to discuss the relationship between baptism, confirmation, and ordination. But a less complex and a less abstract point is being made. In most churches *the* Ministry is almost entirely conceived of as full-time and professional and the clerics are almost entirely from outside. The celebrant of the Eucharist is almost certainly full-time, professional, from outside. Such a cleric will still most often read the Epistle and the Gospel and will preach. There is no place for women to take any active part. There is a fundamental lack of conviction about the Ministry—except the ministry of the full-time professional from outside. To think of recruitment, selection, and training for a voluntary and part-time ministry is inevitably to question this whole pattern. Without becoming in-bred (especially in a society in which locality as it was is fast changing) we must surely break down this indispensable dependence on the full-time professional man-from-outside, so that at the moment "we have been without a vicar for a year" means in effect "we have been without the ministry"—and means, too, "we have been brought up to regard the full-time man from outside coming and living amongst us and being our temporary head as indispensable, and now we are lost without such a person". We must work towards a situation in which no longer is the worship and witness of the Church entirely dependent on such a man. This can only mean working towards a pattern of ministry in which *all* who are in the Church through Christian Initiation are trained for ministry, *continue* to be trained for ministry—for varieties of ministry, varied because of the different gifts and capacities of the members of the Church, and varied because of the different tasks which the Body of Christ needs to have done, for its own sake and for the sake of the world. The local church will require the help of people from outside—teachers, theologians, administrators, etc.; these may or may not be priests, they may or may not be full-time, they may or may not be men. It will take all sorts to make the Church; but the ordained priest, the celebrant of the Eucharist, the preacher, the teacher, the theologian, the administrator, will not *necessarily* be the full-time professional from outside.

It will not be easy to knit into a team those who are on church pay and those who are on secular pay, those who have university qualifications and those who are not so equipped intellectually. It never has been. But here is another opportunity for the Church's words on fellowship to be more than words.

It is at this point necessary to make clear that what has been outlined is no erosion of the nature of ordination. It is a repudiation of the inevitable association of ordination with the full-time professional ministry. Its classic expression is in fact to be found in R. C. Moberly's *Ministerial Priesthood*, published in 1897—which Anthony Hanson describes in his recent book *The Pioneer Ministry* (making a penetrating criticism and appreciation of Moberly) as "so scriptural a conception".

Moberly writes (quoting Charles Gore, *The Church and the Ministry*):

> It is an abuse of the sacerdotal conception, if it is supposed that the priesthood exists to celebrate sacrifices or acts of worship in the place of the body of the people or as their substitute... "*We* bless the cup of blessing"; "*We* break the bread", says St Paul, speaking for the community; "*We* offer" "*We* present" is the language of the liturgies. But the ministry is the organ—the necessary organ—of these functions. It is the hand which offers and distributes ... (p. 71).

He discusses "the relation of ministers specifically ordained, to this total life and power of the total Body".

> ... Clearly they are not intermediaries between the Body and its life ... But they are organs of the Body, though which the life, inherent in the total Body, expresses itself in particular functions of detail. They are organs of the whole Body, working organically for the whole Body, specifically representative for specific purposes and processes of the power of the life, which is the life of the whole Body, not the life of some of its organs. They are for public purposes the organs of the Body's life; but the great life itself, the great deposit of the spiritual life remains in the Body at large (p. 68).

Following up what he has written (all the quotations so far are from Chapter III "The Relations between Ministry and Laity") with a chapter on "The Basis of Ministry—Divine Commission", he begins

5—M

We think, then, of ministry not as a holy intermediary, wielding powers peculiar and inherent, because, it is Spirit-endowed on behalf of those who are not. But Christian ministry is the instrument which represents the whole Spirit-endowed Body of the Church; and yet withal is itself so Spirit-endowed as to have the right and the power to represent instrumentally. The immense exaltation—and requirement—of lay Christianity, which in respect of its own dignity cannot be exaggerated, in no way detracts from the distinctive dignity of the duties which belong to ministerial function, or from the solemn significance of separation to ministry (p. 99).

He then asks: "Of what nature is that which makes such ministerial distinction between the few and the many?" And he answers his own question: "The work is God's work, and the authority to undertake it must be God's authority." And he outlines (p. 105) three ways whereby the Divine Commission may be conveyed: (*a*) directly, through the individual conscience; (*b*) through the general Church body, but without reference to any particular "ministerial" method, or continuity, of transmission; (*c*) from those who have themselves received authority to commission. To insist on the first form alone, he says, would mean setting aside the principle that the Church should be an organized Body at all. The second contains within it the seeds of a congregationalism and sectarianism which could quickly destroy the unity of the Body. The third form—so long as those who have received authority to commission are not conceived as appointed by Christ without reference to the Church, so long indeed as they are not given an authority which does not belong to the rest of the Church and which the rest of the Church can neither give nor take away from them—is, as Anthony Hanson points out, the form which makes him who receives this authority the fittest representative of the whole Church, as indeed the Church of South India has recognized.

This pattern of recruitment for the ministry is of course already most clearly evident when the Church fills up the "higher orders" of the ordained ministry. The Church does not expect someone to volunteer, saying: "I have had a growing conviction that I must offer myself for the episcopate." The Church makes known to the person concerned that she judges the man to be the right man for this office and order. The man may refuse. But the Divine Commission is made known to him through the Church. The Church does not hesitate to confront him. She does not through oblique methods try to stimulate a response from him. She does not watch and wait until the first spark of a response appears in him, and then fan it to a flame. She assesses her needs, and assesses who may be best qualified to meet them. So the Church deals with the question of vocation to one part of the ordained ministry of the Body. Why then should the Church's practice be so different when it comes to the question of vocation to the "inferior" orders?

What then, practically, are we suggesting?

1. That in addition to the present method of recruitment for ordained ministry which relies primarily on the call subjectively experienced, recruitment for the ministry should be woven into the whole structure of the local church. For this to be more than a pious hope, the local congregation will need some regular inescapable confrontation. For instance: each year at a special meeting of the congregation (for example, at Whitsuntide) the whole congregation should be called together to consider who—if any—should be nominated to the bishop from the parish or electoral roll as candidates for the ordained ministry. After nomination, candidates would go to a selection board. There they would merely be selected for *training* for ordained ministry.

2. Unless such a method of recruitment were based upon a pattern of training for ministry for *all*, in which we specify what is involved in ministry, it would be all too easy either for those nominated for ordination to be the kind of ordinand who is already a full-time cleric in embryo or for no one to be nominated, since the people would be looking for a full-time professional. Training of the whole *laos* is therefore intimately related to the first suggestion. At the moment Training for Ministry in the diocese is often extremely uncoordinated —confirmation training and post-confirmation training, lay training centre work, training groups for industrial mission, training for Readers, pre-ordination and post-ordination training, Marriage Guidance, etc., all too often exist in their separate departments or depend on the "genius" of particular people. *Each diocese should have a Diocesan Committee for Training for Ministry*, and the diocesan committee should be related to a central training for ministry committee, which should review the training facilities, methods, and syllabi of each diocese.

3. There will need to be training centres and various types of training; but this means, as we have said, specifying what is involved in ministry. Besides the specialist ministries—industrial ministry, pri-

sons, hospitals, schools, universities, shops, etc.—there will undoubtedly be a great need of assistance in the general ministry of the
local church—ministering in one particular area, or with one particular group. (The development of the house church can easily force
the unassisted priest to spend too much time celebrating the sacrament when there are other important tasks to be done, other
sacraments to be administered.)

4. It is impossible to suggest patterns of training which will be
appropriate for all the diverse areas and people of the Anglican Communion. Nevertheless, it is clear from reports from the different
provinces that *once the intention to encourage voluntary and part-time
ministries is firm means of training are found.*

These suggestions would, I believe, answer the objection which is
sometimes made that to encourage the idea of priests who are also
workers, manual or clerical, would be inevitably to corrupt the concept of the laity and to give way to a defective and over-clericalized
theology of the ministry.[1] This objection must be treated very
seriously. It is undoubtedly a danger if the primary preoccupation
is with "priests" and not with the whole Body of Christ which
"expresses itself in particular functions of detail" as Moberly says,
through its ordained ministry.

There is one other and important reason for encouraging voluntary
and part-time ministries at the moment. Few can doubt that the
Anglican Church, like many other ecclesiastical institutions, is not
only now too clerical—it is that. It is also too bureaucratic. For
instance, liturgy, if it is to be close to life, will not be renewed by liturgical commissions dominated by clerics—full-time and professional.
We need ministries of exploration and experiment. We need new life
and power manifesting itself at and from "ground level". The voluntary and part-time minister with his independence of pay from the
Church could well be a new and powerful force within the Church.
Even to mention this aspect of the subject is, of course, to risk the
subject itself. "Loyalty" is a word that can be too often on the lips of
the hierarchy—meaning loyalty to the hierarchy rather than to the
truth of vision and experience. The ordination of self-supporting laymen to sacramental functions could go a long way to destroy the
stranglehold of clerical bureaucracy. Men whose mentality and
security have been formed and maintained over many years in a
clerical system will, of course, instinctively fear the ordination of

persons who remain in secular employment. But the ordination of secularly employed men may be for this and for many other reasons one of the Church's great advances in our time.

NOTE

1. E. R. Wickham, Bishop of Middleton, *Encounter with Modern Society* (Lutterworth Press, 1964), Chapter 8.

6

The Diaconate

BISHOP OF ST ANDREWS

The 1958 Lambeth Conference was aware that if the diaconate is as important as we say, then our use of it needs to be put on a better footing. Consideration of the subject had been going on quite widely for years. But no clear new picture had been emerging; and the Conference was also aware that a growth of lay ministries that was widely valued might be thrown into confusion unnecessarily if the recovery of the diaconate was wrongly handled. The Conference saw that an important decision would have to be made, but that it should not be attempted until more thinking and work had been done. Therefore Resolution No. 88 was passed:

> The Conference recommends that each province of the Anglican Communion shall consider whether the office of Deacon shall be restored to its primitive place as a distinctive order in the Church, instead of being regarded as a probationary period for the priesthood.

And the report of the Committee (p. 2/106 f) included the following opinion:

> that the time has come to clarify the whole structure of lay ministries in relation to the Order of Deacon.

The Conference of 1968 will have to consider whether firm answers can yet be given. In the intervening years study and experiment have increased on a wide front. Within the Anglican Communion progress has been as much by discovering what does not promise well as in discovering what does. The contribution of the World Council of Churches has been to draw into the debate a wide range of traditions. A decisive step has been taken by the Roman Catholic Church and they are restoring a permanent diaconate. The pattern has similarity to some of our own experiments, and those not always very successful. The Roman development will be watched with sympathy and hope.

Deliberation about the diaconate is still cramped by lack of comprehensive and thorough studies. Much of the best work is hidden away in reports and articles. Nevertheless, to follow the diaconate through its history and transformations is important for any assessment of the road to restoration. It may therefore be convenient to begin this paper with a brief historical review which may serve to outline some of the more important perspectives.

Deacons in the New Testament

Deacons existed in the days of the apostles (Phil. 1.1; 1 Tim. 3.8–9); and that the order was started by the apostles is not seriously questioned. The way in which the diaconate began is less certain. Some have suggested it was a development from the mission of the seventy. Farrer has urged that such "households" as that of Stephanas (1 Cor. 16) throw light on the beginnings;[1] but the appointment of the Seven (Acts 6) by the apostles is still the most generally accepted evidence, and to this our ordinals lend their support. However, we must proceed with care.

The Acts of the Apostles has no specific reference to deacons, although it was written later than the Pauline epistles, which have. In Acts 6.1–6 it is not actually said that the Seven who were ordained were deacons, a point to which St John Chrysostom first drew attention in the fourth century.[2] On the other hand, the early Church acknowledged the identification, and St Irenaeus (c.180), who knew both East and West, accepts it without question. At the very least this means that the second-century Church had no difficulty in identifying what it read in Acts 6 with what it knew by tradition and experience of the office of a deacon. That the diaconate in the second century was probably already beginning to diverge from the mundane functions described in Acts only adds weight to the identification.

It is highly unlikely that the apostles said, "Let us create an order of deacons." In a small community that was growing so that twelve men in Jerusalem could no longer undertake every ministration, they took a step whereby a subordinate and derived ministry was created to carry part of the load. The prayer and laying on of hands indicate that the Seven were provided with authority and grace. The tendency must be resisted to set this event in a context of local churches and a threefold ministry. That came soon after, when a spreading Church

called forth a Christian presbyterate. It is likely that at first the
deacons' ministry as assistants to the apostles expanded as the apostles
became increasingly occupied, and this may account for Philip
preaching and baptizing a few weeks later. Then with the development of the presbyterate the diaconate would adjust again to make
room for it. The Christendom of Irenaeus was different from that
of Acts 6, and so the diaconate had not exactly identical shape.
Christendom of today is different again, and the functions of the
Seven, or of a "primitive diaconate" will not give an accurate
picture of what a contemporary diaconate should be. It is more
profitable to ask what the primitive diaconate *was*, than what particular deacons *did*.

1. Like all followers of Christ they were servants, but characteristically they were associated with that special ministry of service which
was the apostolic mission to mankind. The diaconate was located in
the lower, mundane levels of that ministry. Theirs was not so much a
special mission as a responsibility to carry such humbler loads as
would free the apostolic mission for its principal work. They were
there to do what might be needed at the time.

2. Yet this humbler service gives them an almost symbolic place in
the Church. That they are essentially and in name "servants"
relates them to what every Christian is about, whether he is apostle,
layman, or deacon. We cannot remind ourselves too often that deacon,
servant, and minister are all translations of the one Greek word
diakonos. Moreover in New Testament references to Christian
character *diakonos* and *doulos* (slave) are often used interchangeably.
The thought of the Suffering Servant, faithful to death, is not far
away, and the death of Stephen gives a startling emphasis to this
extreme significance. The universal importance of the Seven, and of
deacons, is that they were dedicated to humble service, not that they
were clergymen. This esteem for the servant, with all its Christian
overtones, makes sense of the otherwise extravagant language of St
Ignatius (*c.*105): "Let all men respect the deacons as Jesus Christ."[3]

3. They were ordained men. To the contemporary outlook the most
surprising thing about the Seven is that they were ordained at all.
To serve tables would seem to be what any Christian layman might
be doing. The apostles saw it differently. The implication may be that
for dedication to a specific work of Christian service the adequate
equipment is blessing by God and commissioning by the Church.

4. All the indications are that the ministry of the Seven was flexible and adaptable. Not only does the little we know of Stephen and Philip support this, but also the passage the diaconate accomplished in moving from being the whole subordinate ministry in the earliest days to its place in the threefold ministry of Ignatius and Cyprian tells the same story.

The early Church

As the Church grew, the general pattern of ministry for each locality was the bishop with his presbyters and his deacons. But this was not a simple three-grade arrangement. Presbyters and deacons were different species, each related directly to the bishop. Diagrammatically it might be put thus:

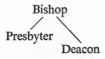

Although inferior to the presbyters, the deacons had a close relation to the bishop, reflecting the relation of the Seven to the apostles. They were the bishop's men. Hippolytus (*c.*200) lays great stress on this in his account of the ordination rite:

> Nevertheless we order that the bishop alone shall lay on hands at the ordaining of a deacon for this reason: that he is not ordained for priesthood, but for the service of the bishop that he may do the things commanded by him.[4]

An extension of this outlook was later to produce the archdeacon.

The activities of deacons were diverse in the early Church. In Hippolytus's ordination rite the only function referred to is a liturgical one—an ominous indication, perhaps, that already the surplice was exerting a lure. But elsewhere there is evidence of deacons as bishops' messengers, secretaries, or ambassadors, as guardians or instructors of catechumens, as disbursers of the Church's alms, as protectors of orphans and searchers for the sick, as models of piety, and even as beachcombers who sought the corpses of mariners and provided decent burial.

Inside the church deacons looked after the congregation, keeping them in order and leading them in the prayers. They read lections in the liturgy and presented the offertory gifts. They joined in administering Communion to the faithful, and also took the Sacrament to those who were not present. They did not celebrate the Eucharist, but they did baptize and preach, though more often in times of special need than as a general thing.

The list varies with time and place. In some places deacons were numerous, in others—including Rome—their number was restricted to seven, in a misguided following of Acts. Seven deacons who were "bishop's men" and had the episcopal ear tended to become an influential inner group. The emphasis in Acts on humble service was fading. Other evidence of this is all too easy to find. Repeatedly in the fourth century Councils passed canons designed to check the presumption of deacons. For example, they are not to put themselves among the presbyters, not to go up to Communion first, and the Council of Nicaea even found it necessary to underline that they were not competent to celebrate.

Increasingly the liturgical aspect of the diaconate became predominant and typical, and zeal for caring for widows and running canteens fell away. Humble duties still needed to be done, and minor orders arose partly to fill the gap, though as time went on those too clambered after the dignity of hierarchy.

This early distortion of the diaconate through concentration on status and liturgical functions must not be forgotten. And it is of a piece with an observation Congar has made on the Ministry as a whole:

> The concept of ministry seems to have undergone, between its origins and now, two successive reductions or contractions: from service as something universal to institutional ministries or hierarchies; and then from institutional ministries to the ministry of priesthood alone. It is this last which we mean when we speak of "*the* ministry".[5]

Apart from the element of decline, we may consider also that the diversity of diaconal activity in the early Church, in a world very different from our own, indicates that we shall not discover the shape for a contemporary diaconate by asking what those deacons did and expecting a clear and perennially valid answer.

Medieval and modern

Increasingly the medieval diaconate took its character and status from the fact of belonging to the hierarchy; and increasingly the hierarchy's distinctive function was to celebrate Mass. This the deacon could not do, and so the order steadily ceased to have any significant existence.

Parishes and oratories wanted priests, and the pastoral deacon was seldom acceptable as a substitute. He could assist the priest liturgically and pastorally, but efforts (as by Bishop Grossteste of Lincoln) to have deacons on the staff of every parish made little headway. A man contemplating celibacy and a pastoral ministry was more likely to consider his vocation was to the priesthood. With the diaconate become the low rung in a *cursus honorum*, and its function some ill-defined auxiliary occupation, few men made it a life's work. In some dioceses deacons were attached to the cathedral, but a later tendency to appoint cantors restricted that opening. Except for the office of archdeacon the diaconate in the West was a mere penultimate step on the road to priesthood.

In the East change was slower, but the permanent deacon has become rare, and his duties are usually to do with liturgical music. Most deacons are on the way to becoming priests, and are deacons for only a few weeks; but some able and unmarried men may remain deacons for years, serving meanwhile as personal secretaries and liturgical assistants to the bishop. From such future bishops are chosen.

In the West the Reformation did not work a transformation. The episcopal Churches zealously retained the order of deacons, but used it only as a formal preliminary to priesthood. The Roman deacon remained in his seminary: the Anglican tested his wings in a parish. Few Anglicans remained deacons for more than the necessary year or two, the exceptions being mostly men whose ordination served to qualify them for a college fellowship.

In the Lutheran and Calvinist Churches there was a measure of restoration,[6] though less than some of the principal reformers themselves proposed. The tendency was for interest to concentrate more on a diaconal activity than on deacons as an order. This activity took the form of care for the poor, the sick, and others in distress, either by individuals appointed by the Church, or by the Christian community itself. In some quarters there was a line of development whereby deacons were those with responsibility for the alms, and so for the finances, of the congregations. The concept of deaconing as service had a strong revival in Continental Lutheranism in the early nineteenth century under the leadership of Johann Wichern and others. Work which began among the abandoned youth of Hamburg grew to social, missionary, and pastoral work of wide extent. Those engaged in the work came to be called deacons and deaconesses, and they belonged to institutions or communities (Bruderhäuser). Today in Germany there are 4,500 deacons, and 15 Bruderhäuser which provide professional training, largely for state examinations and appointments. The system is not an integrally constituted part of the Church, and the deacons are not ordained, nor have they any particular place in the local congregation.

Recent History

The twentieth century is witnessing a widespread concern to recover for the ministry of the Church a real diaconate.[7] Frequently the objective is seen as a restoration of "permanent deacons", that is of an order of ministry, with recognizably distinct functions, to which a man could find a vocation for life, meanwhile perhaps earning his living in some other way. In recent years several Anglican provinces have made provision for permanent deacons. Action "in the near future" was promised in the Church of England in 1929.

Some of the main reasons for intensified interest in the diaconate are (*a*) that the uses to which Churches today put this ministry are plainly open to criticism; (*b*) ecumenical dialogue, which causes Churches to examine their own accepted practices; (*c*) the belief that if the Church has three orders of ministry it must be injurious for one order to exist only nominally; (*d*) the shortage of clergy, and the possibility of part-time clergy; (*e*) the need, with the increasing practice of frequent Communion, for ministers who can assist the celebrant in the administration at the Eucharist.

Too often the pressure of a particular need has developed a tendency to set up a permanent diaconate to do this or that particular thing, whereas any restoration should be based on a broader study of what the diaconate is and what deacons are for.

Experience of a revived, permanent diaconate has, so far, shown only limited success. Here and there in Africa and in parts of the U.S.A. there is progress, but more generally the picture seems to be that on closer examination bishops feel it would complicate rather than help their situation; or if experiments have been tried they have not accomplished very much. If a few dioceses are left out of the reckoning, the total number of permanent deacons in the Anglican Communion today is quite small.

In Scotland an experiment has been approved,[8] but not yet started, which concentrates more than most on the town parish, and locates the diaconate in a number of people carrying out a variety of largely "lay" services in support of the priest's ministry of Word and Sacraments.

In Asia the Church of South India[9] has pressed for further study of the diaconate. A committee of the C.I.P.B.C., having reviewed available experience, reaffirms the importance of revitalizing the diaconate, but does not see the answer in current notions of permanent diaconate:

> The proposal for "permanent deacons" has not been taken up with any enthusiasm in the Anglican Communion as a whole, and in this province the practice of the several dioceses and the replies of the bishops to our queries show that opinion is almost unanimously unfavourable.[10]

The movement of the Roman Catholic Church can be traced from discussions in Dachau concentration camp where Wilhelm Schamoni was a prisoner, and from the critical need of clergy in South America, to the Pope's *motu proprio* of 6 July 1967 "Regulations for Permanent Diaconate". The Vatican Council said:

> In communion with the bishop and his group of priests they serve in the diaconate of the liturgy, of the word, and of charity to the People of God.[11]

These three functions, liturgical, pastoral, and charitable, can be followed into the *motu proprio*, though there the liturgical and sacramental activities are enumerated most. Only provinces that want them need have these deacons. The majority of the deacons will be celibate, their training will normally take three years, they may have another occupation, they are of the hierarchy, and they are deacons for life.

Retrospect

Out of all this history certain points deserve special attention.

1. Accepting Acts 6 as a general starting-point for the diaconate, the task given the Seven is seen to have a considerable *ad hoc* element. They were to do what was wanted then and there and in that situation. This points to flexibility and adaptability.

2. As the name *diakonos* implies, their characteristic is Christian service.

3. That, for the purposes of running a charity, they were ordained at all can be very surprising by present ideas. Two conclusions follow: (*a*) that influenced by current studies of laity we are underestimating the need for grace and the manifest backing of the Church for those carrying particular Christian responsibilities; and (*b*) that we are reading into Acts more ideas of ordination than the text requires: public commissioning and a blessing might cover what was done.

4. When a diaconate of humble service is absent, compensating ministries arise to fill the gap. Thus, when in the early days the deacons concentrated on a liturgical way of life, the minor orders arose to do what any deacon could have been doing. When later the diaconate rated as a temporary incident on the road to priesthood, then have arisen catechists, lay readers, teachers, administrators, Bible women, and others to fill the gap again. Without denying that the diaconate is of the Ministry, one may suspect that an error is made whenever it is associated exclusively with hierarchy and the clergy.

5. History does not provide any adequate warrant for our present use of the diaconate as the final year or so before priesthood. This is now widely conceded.[12] Others go further and assert that not only is it a misuse but an inept one: the qualification for a probationary ministry should not be a permanent and indelible order.

6. Most studies of the diaconate still stress the need for a liturgical element as expressing that side of Christian service which is the worship of God. But it is doubtful if what, over all, the Church is about is altered if every ministry of service and every deacon does not have a particular liturgical place.

7. An analysis of why recent attempts to recover a permanent diaconate have not made better progress points to the following causes:

(*a*) In matters of training, status, and (especially liturgical) function—besides stoles, collars, and titles—we still require it to approximate too closely to what goes with priesthood. In consequence, not only does a man choose priesthood rather than diaconate, but the permanent deacon frequently wants to become a priest.

(*b*) On the other hand, many of the things that are often assigned to a revised diaconate are already being done by laymen; lay people are catechists and readers, they administer the chalice, they visit, they are welfare officers, and so on. In this case the deacon is duplicating the lay ministry, so why ordain him, or why not ordain them? We do not want to change the active laity into clergy. And what would happen to the women?

(*c*) Increasingly it has become apparent in most parts of the world that the shortage of clergy is pre-eminently a shortage of priests. When the need is for ministers who can celebrate the Eucharist, an auxiliary ministry of part-time priests will have more attraction than permanent deacons can ever have.

Prospects: some possible courses

Since 1958 concern to recover the diaconate has spread, but there is no general agreement yet about the way it should be done, and there is some opinion that any worth-while development is unlikely. Possible courses facing the 1968 Conference include these:

1. The diaconate could be deliberately dropped, and a twofold ministry asserted. This course cuts across all the Anglican Church and its ordinal have maintained for so long about the threefold ministry of the Catholic Church. On the other hand, it might be said to face the truth that for centuries now we have existed with, in fact, only two orders, the use we have made of the diaconate being at best notional and at worst a subterfuge.

2. While discarding our present use of the diaconate as a preliminary to priesthood, we could continue study and experiments, in the expectation that in due time illumination will come through experience and the whole developing ecumenical process and study.

3. We could continue with experiments, meanwhile retaining our present diaconate to provide a thread of continuity into the future.

To these main alternatives another line of thought might be added. The present problem may be not so much to recover and restore a true diaconate as to identify and locate it, as being already in existence. We have noticed that one hindrance to proposals for a permanent diaconate is that they duplicate activity that already exists in the Church. That duplication possibly indicates that a real diaconal ministry is already in being. It exists in the catechists, readers, dedicated nurses, welfare workers, secretaries, and other "lay ministries".

To ordain these men and women, we have already noted, would

undo all we have learned about active Christian service and turn them all into ministers. Yet we license readers and catechists, often with a service of blessing; we commission stewardship leaders, and have various and valued services of dedication for undertakings of real Christian responsibility. This may not be much different from the kind of "making" the seven deacons had. And if we are disposed to say that such "lay" ministries are better without any sort of commissioning or blessing in the name of the Church, we then have to face the fact that the apostles did lay hands on their charity administrators.

Such commissionings ("ordinations" has too many acquired associations to use it here, though it would be a proper word) plainly could not be for life in most instances, but for a suitable period of years, or for the time required for a particular undertaking. Possibly a source of difficulty in plans to restore the diaconate has been the very assumption that it must be permanent. For the twentieth century the contrary may be true. Even if the apostles intended to make permanent deacons (and it is not certain that they did), the nature of the diaconate as flexible and existing for contemporary need could require it to be different in many parts of the world now.

If the order of deacon is lifelong and with indelible character, there is no point in contemplating short-term diaconal ministries. But there is some room for reconsideration. Orders are for life on two grounds. First the Church has traditionally wished to treat them so: and this ruling the Church may be competent to revise, especially in the case of an order that was founded by the apostolic ministry and is not dominical. Second, orders are indelible. This, if it is correct, the Church cannot change; but the theology of indelible character as applicable to holy orders has only a short history prior to the Council of Florence (1438).[13] The question may well be considered still open at least as concerns diaconate.

The people whom we have suggested are today already fulfilling the diaconal ministry of service—who are the diaconate—include many women. Are they to be seen as deaconesses, and the female counterpart of deacons? The traditional debates about whether deaconesses are "in orders" comparable to deacons lose much of their force when we concentrate on deacons as being essentially servants, and less as being semi-sacerdotal. We are regarding deacons as persons "upon whom hands are imposed 'not unto the priesthood, but unto a ministry of service'".[14] The New Testament does not speak of "deaconesses" (*diakonissa*—a fourth-century word): Phoebe is "a servant (*ousan diakonon*) of the church that is at Cenchreae" (Rom. 16.1, R.V.). Hence Lightfoot's opinion:

> As I read my New Testament, the female diaconate is as definite an institution as the male diaconate. Phoebe is as much a deacon as Stephen or Philip is a deacon.[15]

Training for this diaconate would be, and is, diverse. Following the present line of thought it is clear that the kinds of dedicated service comprised within the diaconate would be numerous, in a single diocese, and as between continents. Catechists would need some theological training; for a nurse professional competence would be a required qualification; and for all the quality of life would have pre-eminence.

One might envisage a "making of deacons" as a routine and simple service in a local church, or in the cathedral, much as lay readers or women workers are blessed and licensed now. People would be licensed by the bishop specifically for the service they were to do, and for differing terms of years. Among them could be ordinands licensed for a year or two's probation in a parish, after which they might be ordained priest. In most parts of the world, at such a making of deacons, complete simplicity and lack of trappings would be suitable. The familiar accompaniments of ordinations would too readily revive the curse of the diaconate—the withdrawal from the circumstances of lay life, and a restless feeling that it is not reason that they should serve tables, and that the Church should find some other men of good repute to appoint over that business.

July 1967

NOTES

1. *The Apostolic Ministry*, pp. 142 ff.
2. *Hom. on Acts* XIV.
3. *Trall.* 3.
4. *The Apostolic Tradition*, ed. Gregory Dix, p. 15.
5. *Le Diacre*, ed. Winninger and Yves Congar (1966), p. 125.
6. See World Council Studies No. 2 "The Ministry of Deacons", 1965.
7. See the report of the World Council of Churches Consultation, "The Ministry of Deacons in the Church", 1964.
8. Report "Deacons and the Church", 1963.
9. Report by Synod Theological Commission, 1964.

10. Report "Ministries and Manpower" (1965), p. 13.
11. *De Ecclesia*, 29; cf. *Ad Gentes*, 16, and *Orientalum Ecclesiarum*, 17.
12. For example, C.S.I. report in n.9 above; also Karl Rahner in *Le Diacre* (see n.5 above), p. 211.
13. Cf. Joseph Bingham, *Antiquities*, Vol. VIII, Part II, 6.6.
14. Vatican II, *De Ecclesia*, 29.
15. J. B. Lightfoot, Primary Charge, quoted in "The Ministry of Women", a report to the Archbishop of Canterbury (1919), p. 11.

7

Women and the Priesthood

ALAN RICHARDSON

The recent Report on *Women and Holy Orders* (C.I.O., 1966) made it clear that irreconcilable views are held within the Church of England upon this subject. How strongly the views of the opposed parties are represented amongst the clergy and the laity it is impossible to say, since the Commission had no means of conducting a sociological opinion-survey. The impression (it can be no more than that) left upon some members of the Commission is that, although there are strong and vociferous parties on each side, the vast majority of church people are apathetic and have never given serious consideration to the question of the ordination of women to the priesthood. This is why it seemed wise to give attention to the question of the diaconate (the word "deacon" in Greek is common gender) and to the wider question of the redeployment of the laity. But this part of the Report has received little attention in the press or in discussions amongst church members, and it does not primarily concern us here.

Pseudo-theological considerations

It is sometimes said that there are no theological objections to the ordination of women to the priesthood. (It is reasonable to ask what, if anything, would constitute a valid theological objection in this sense.) Sometimes what is meant is that there are no valid *logical* objections; for instance, if it is said that women can have no place in the priesthood because Christ did not appoint a woman apostle, it could be logically replied that Christ did not appoint a Gentile apostle, and that therefore no Gentile has been validly ordained priest or consecrated bishop. On a similar level is the argument that women cannot become priests because the incarnation occurred in a male person; since the incarnation took place in the person of a Jew, the same reasoning would seem to exclude Gentiles from the priest-

hood. Similarly, the fact that priestesses have in the past been associated with pagan and polytheistic cults with their magical fertility
rites has no logical bearing on the totally different biblical-Christian
concept of priesthood. Again, arguments from the so-called "male
principle" in the universe will carry little weight with those familiar
with contemporary thinking in the sphere of linguistic philosophy. If
such arguments are advanced as "theological" in character, they will
discredit theology as a serious means of understanding the human
situation in relation to our universe.

Theological considerations

Nevertheless, there are serious theological arguments for and against
the ordination of women to the priesthood. The most important of
these concern the nature of priesthood itself. If one holds the popular
Protestant conception of the "priesthood of all believers", there is no
reason at all why women should not be ordained, since there is no
distinctively priestly function; ordination is only a matter of due and
seemly appointment to an office in the congregation. If, on the other
hand, one holds the biblical doctrine that the whole Church is
priestly, offering up the Christian sacrifice of the Body of Christ, then
the priest at his ordination is made the representative man through
whom the priestly offering of the people is presented to God. It would
be hard to find any biblical grounds why women should not perform
this priestly offering, if the Church decided to admit them to the Order
of Priests. Women are already, equally with men, members of the
People of God, "kings and priests unto God". To object to their
ordination on the grounds that men can represent men *and* women
but that women can represent only women (the so-called Pauline
Principle) is to raise dubious questions which cannot have verifiable
answers; the main truth is that women, equally with men, are human
beings whom Christ has come to redeem. Thus, on the biblical view
that the whole *laos* or laity is priestly, a woman who had been duly
ordained by the decision of the historic Church in the fullness of its
ecumenical authority could validly celebrate the Eucharist.

The question, however, remains, whether such a decision taken by
a single separate branch of the Church (for example, the Anglican
Communion) could possess such authority; it would not be reverting
to an ancient practice (as, for example, restoring the Cup to the laity),
but would be making an innovation for which there was no ancient

or ecumenical precedent. This is the crucial question which underlies the debate whether the Anglican Communion should proceed to the ordination of women to the priesthood now. It is a profoundly theological question, since it raises the issue of authority in the separated branches of the universal Church of Christ. It goes much deeper than discussions about whether such unilateral action would help or hinder progress towards organic unity amongst the Churches. Doubtless such questions are important and they ought to be carefully considered, but the fundamental question concerns the theological propriety of an innovation within one branch of the historic Church, lacking the consensus of the whole Church.

Pastoral considerations

If it were granted that a woman could validly be made a priest in the Church of God (and there would seem to be no theological reasons why she should not be, if the fullness of the Church's authority so determined), there would still remain the pastoral question. A woman duly ordained to the priesthood could validly minister the Word and Sacraments, but in the nature of the case she could not be a father-in-God to the people of a parish or a diocese. A woman instituted as rector or vicar of a parish could not be the head of the family in the same way that Christ is head of the Church. She could not be the representative *persona*, or at least not in the same sense as a man can be. If the so-called Pauline Principle (cf. Eph. 5.22) has any validity at all, this is the point at which it is applicable. But it can be argued that, though a woman-rector would have a different pastoral relation to her flock from that of her male counterpart, it could be a valuable enrichment of the Church's life; there is room for "a mother in Israel" as well as for the father-figure. Arguments on this subject are inconclusive. All that can be done here is to point out that the pastorate of the woman parish priest would be *different* (not necessarily better or worse) from that of a man. Perhaps it would be complementary.

Sociological considerations

As far as the Church of England is concerned (however it may be in other provinces of the Anglican Communion), the true character of the Church's ministry has been obscured and distorted by the mono-

polization of ministry by a professional priesthood. Certain specialized functions are reserved to the episcopate, but the diaconate has
been divested of almost all significance. This misdevelopment has
created in the minds of church people, clergy and laity alike, the
impression that the professional priesthood is the only real form of
ministry; hence the assumption that women, if they are to have a
genuine share in the ministry, must be ordained to the professional
priesthood. The misdevelopment (so strangely contrasted with the
ministry in the apostolic Church, in which there were no professionals)
can be understood readily enough in the light of English social history, but the problem which it has bequeathed to our age is that of
the place and function of a professional priesthood at a time when
the social conditions which created it are rapidly passing away. For
this reason many of the clergy today feel uncertain of their place and
function in society, and some of them consequently seek to find
employment outside the parochial system. To ordain women as priests
merely because the parochial ministry cannot be kept going as a
result of the shortage of manpower would be the worst of all possible
reasons for the innovation.

The underlying difficulty is, of course, not sociological at all; it is
basically the result of a failure to reach a proper understanding of the
Church's priestly ministry. There are, in the last resort, no "non-
theological factors" in issues of this kind; behind every sociological
or psychological development there is a theological issue. The theology of priesthood, whether of men or of women, is where the discussion of the Church's ministry should begin—and end. It is not
merely for sociological reasons that the ministry of the Word and
Sacraments cannot be indefinitely sustained by a monopolistic professional class, even though that class is enlarged by the ordination of
women to the priesthood. It cannot be sustained upon theological
grounds. This is why the concentration of attention upon the question
of the ordination of women to the priesthood is mistaken; it diverts
the mind of the Church from the more important question of the
nature and function of an ordained ministry in a secular society.

8

The Nature of
the Anglican Episcopate

R. P. C. HANSON

The justification for episcopacy as it is preserved within the Anglican Communion is, and always has been, perfectly clear, though it is not perhaps one that would satisfy the doctrinaire mind. It rests upon three propositions:

1. The Anglican Churches inherited an episcopal form of government from the late medieval Church.

2. They regarded this form of ministry as agreeable to the Word of God as it is found in the Scriptures, and the actual holders of episcopal office during the reigns of Henry VIII, Edward VI, and Elizabeth I either encouraged a Reformation according to the Word of God or did not render such a Reformation impossible.

3. The Anglican Churches therefore believed that they had no authority to alter the episcopal form of government.

To put the same propositions theologically, the justification for Anglican episcopacy is tradition found to be agreeable to the Scriptures. One of the most remarkable features of the work of early Anglican apologists, such as Jewel and Hooker, is that they make no serious attempt to claim that the episcopal form of government is set forth in the New Testament as the exclusively authoritative pattern of ministry. All that they claim is that it is to be found in Scripture and is not repugnant to the Word of God. And they stress the authority which it derives from having been adopted for well over a thousand years by the universal Church. They do not of course commend any other form of ministry as scriptural, far less as *more* scriptural. But they do not rest the claim of episcopacy solely on the authority of

Scripture. In thus deliberately emphasizing the authority of tradition (but tradition consonant with Scripture) they were reproducing a feature of Anglicanism which is fundamental to its whole nature. But the early Anglican divines make it quite clear that they do not regard episcopacy as an *articulus stantis aut cadentis ecclesiae*. Where episcopal government can be preserved and had, there not only *might* it be adopted but there it *should* be adopted. They recognize candidly that at the time of the Reformation in the sixteenth century there were certain Reformed Churches which were simply unable to effect a Reformation without sacrificing episcopal government; they had to choose between bishops with no Reformation or Reformation with no bishops. Anglicans do not judge, do not unchurch, these Christian bodies. Such was certainly the judgement of the divines of the sixteenth century, and of most of those of the seventeenth century. This charitable judgement appears to be continued in the use made by Anglican missionary and teaching societies of ministers from Continental non-episcopal Churches in the eighteenth and nineteenth centuries, and in the judgements of several Lambeth Conferences concerning the efficacy of the ministries of non-episcopal Churches, and in the very general co-operation between Anglican Churches and non-episcopal Churches which exists all over the world today. Perhaps one may be permitted to remark that it does appear difficult to imagine that an efficacious ministry could be exercised by ministers whose orders are invalid, unless the word "efficacious" is interpreted very broadly and the word "invalid" very narrowly.

But it should be clear that this view of episcopacy emphatically does not regard episcopacy as a thing indifferent. Where it can be had, there it ought to be had, for it is supported by tradition consonant with Scripture. Anglican Churches have inherited episcopacy, by the providence of God. Though they do not unchurch those Christians who do not possess it, they are bound to try to persuade them to adopt this form of government, and they have no authority to abandon it themselves, even for the sake of Christian unity.

Because of the traditionally pragmatic nature of Anglican thought, it is useful to look at the functioning of episcopal government within the Anglican framework. Episcopacy has in Anglican hands shown itself remarkably flexible and has manifested a surprising power of survival. It has functioned ever since the sixteenth century in a number of very diverse ecclesiastical structures. It has served as an instrument of an absolute or would-be absolute monarchy under Elizabeth I and the Stuart dynasty. Its almost Erastian attachment to the State under the oligarchic government of eighteenth-century England caused many people to think that Anglican bishops, once disestablished, would simply cease to function and just disappear. But the disestablishment of several Anglican Churches during the last two centuries has seen the power and status of the bishops, if anything, enhanced. Bishops co-operated with voluntary societies, allowing them at times much authority, during the growth of the colonial Churches in the nineteenth century and later in independent overseas Churches. Missionary bishops found themselves often compelled to act very much on their own initiative and sometimes to oppose resolutely the action of an imperial government. Some have in some areas gained almost absolute powers in their Churches. But most recently Anglican bishops have functioned effectively as constitutional bishops restrained by a diocesan council and diocesan synod in disestablished Churches or Churches which never had been established and whose structures reflect the influence of contemporary liberal democracy. Anglican bishops have functioned in situations where both secular and ecclesiastical law were uncertain, and in circumstances (as in England since about 1870) when ecclesiastical law had almost completely collapsed. In all these situations the Anglican bishop has not only survived but has adapted himself successfully to the situation.

In moments of reflection, of self-examination, and in periods of uncertainty or in situations where no local precedents existed, he has tended to look to the bishops of the early Church, the Church of the first four centuries, as his model, rather than to expect guidance for specifically episcopal action in the New Testament. Both Ignatius of Antioch and Cyprian of Carthage have been often cited as setting the model for the Anglican bishop. In fact the Anglican episcopacy appears to have Ignatian and Cyprianic elements in its nature but not to be an exact reproduction of the model of episcopacy given by either of these two Fathers. The Ignatian traits are visible in the very strong moral, rather than legal, appeal which the Anglican bishop has always made to the loyalty of his flock, and in the emphasis upon the personal relationship which exists between the bishop and his clergy. The Cyprianic features are the concept that all bishops hold a common responsibility (*in solidum* is Cyprian's phrase) for the whole Church, manifested in the tendency of the bishops of an Anglican province to meet for common counsel, and in the meetings of the Lambeth Conference. Another is the very Cyprianic reluctance visible in the Anglican Communion of one bishop to overrule or another to interfere with his diocese. The Lambeth Conference, after all, does not legislate.

We might perhaps also describe as Cyprianic the tendency of Anglicans to insist upon the apostolic succession of their bishops. Cyprian, of course, believed that our Lord had directly consecrated the apostles as bishops and that they in their turn had directly consecrated bishops (and monepiscopal bishops) as their successors, and that these had continued the succession to his day. Cyprian was perhaps the first Father to express this theory in its simplest form. The earliest Anglican apologists, Jewel and Hooker, clearly do not regard this as an important doctrine. They lived in a period when there were plenty of able scholars ready to dispute this very doubtful theory and in their defence of episcopacy they did not wish to take issue upon this point. But later Anglican writers, during the next two centuries, were not so nice, and this particular theory of apostolic succession reappears frequently in the pages of Anglican apologists. With the advent of the Tractarian Movement in the nineteenth century it not only carried much wider support, but was enhanced among many Anglicans by a new theory of apostolic succession, unknown to the Church of Irenaeus or even of Cyprian. This was a theory of succession of *consecration*. The old theory of succession was one of succession of *office*; each bishop had succeeded his predecessor in office and he his predecessor, and so on back to the apostles. It was also consequently a succession of authority. But this new theory emphasized the handing on of grace of episcopal orders by episcopal consecration, so that the stress was thrown not merely on the fact that a bishop had succeeded to an episcopal predecessor in a see and had inherited his authority, but on the fact that he had been consecrated by bishops and therefore had received a faculty or power to do certain things (such as ordain and confirm) which only bishops, in the nature of things as given by Christ, could do. From this new emphasis in the doctrine of apostolic succession it was a short step to the traditional medieval doctrine that bishops confer an indelible character in consecration, restricted to them alone, and that their function is primarily sacerdotal, that is, they possess the sole legitimate divinely authenticated means of access to grace or to a sacrificial cult. Consonant with this is the view that bishops constitute the

Church and that only through their hierarchical ministry does the work of Christ in the Holy Spirit reach the faithful Christian. Views such as these have never been completely representative of the Anglican Communion, but there is no doubt that since about the year 1850 many Anglicans, clergy and laity, theologians and ordinary men in the pew or the pulpit, have held these views, and that some still do. It is, of course, impossible to regard these theories as consistent with the refusal, already referred to, to condemn those Churches which at the Reformation found it impossible or inexpedient to continue episcopal government.

These views never represented more than a part of Anglican opinion, and recent intellectual and ecclesiastical developments, such as the rise of historical criticism, of "biblical theology", and of the Parish and People Movement, have tended very much to reduce their influence. Historical investigation has made it difficult to believe that the apostles directly instituted monepiscopacy, or that this form of government was universally adopted by the Church earlier than about the middle of the second century; and sacerdotal or hierarchical doctrines of the ministry are manifestly a later development still. But to concede this does not mean that there is no value in the doctrine of the apostolic succession in which bishops of the Anglican Communion stand. This succession is the most striking proof and witness of the historical continuity of the Church, a continuity which goes back to an age when the work and words of the apostles were a living memory. Historical continuity can be expressed in a Church in other ways, such as in the whole parochial organization and institutional integrity such as was maintained (for example) by the Church of Denmark at the time of the Reformation, without its actually retaining episcopal succession, and historical continuity of apostolic succession of bishops alone is no guarantee of soundness of doctrine and vitality in itself alone, as the example of the Ethiopian Church shows. But continuity of episcopal succession is none the less historical continuity manifested in a central feature of the Church's life, and a feature whose existence has remained independent of the changes of culture and sentiment and circumstance which the Church as an institution has experienced through the centuries. It represents continuity in a form of ministry which the Church very early adopted universally and preserved unbroken for at least fourteen hundred years. If the historical continuity of the Church is to have any weight at all—and if we ignore historical continuity, we are faced with grave difficulties in determining the authority of the Church and of the ministry—then clearly this particular form of expression of historical continuity must be valued highly and must distinguish bishops who possess it from other people calling themselves bishops who do not. Above all, the Anglican Churches which have retained this ancient and universal form of expression of historical continuity have no authority to abandon it, and should rather attempt so to explain and commend it to other denominations that they too will be ready to accept it.

If we next ask what is the nature of the authority of the Anglican bishop, we shall have to say that ultimately his authority is a moral authority, based on respect for the tradition of the Church. The fact that at the Reformation, and for some considerable time after, the function and status of the Anglican bishop were intimately involved with the monarchy and the Tudor, Stuart, and Hanoverian polities has now by the same course of history been shown to be a contingent feature of Anglican episcopacy and not an essential one. Anglican bishops have long functioned in a distinctively Anglican way in countries and situations where they had no special connection with the monarchy (if there was one) nor with the State. Indeed, the Anglican bishop has shown that he can function almost without the support of ecclesiastical law. In England since 1870 bishops of the established Church have found it impossible to enforce very large parts of the body of ecclesiastical law which was in existence before the Oxford Movement, and most of which has never been formally repealed. It is a fact worthy of remark that in spite of what appeared to people like Henry Wilberforce and Henry Manning to be the collapse of formal authority in the Church of England in the middle of the last century, the bishops of the Church of England have continued to wield authority, an authority which was in some ways the stronger for being moral and not legal, and which manifestly attached to the office and not the person. On the whole, the Anglican bishop has been averse to invoking the support of law, even when ministering in a Church where ecclesiastical law was accepted and observed, and has preferred to use moral rather than legal suasion. This does not of course imply that Anglican bishops ignore and reject ecclesiastical law and the formal use of their authority in ecclesiastical decisions. Bishops in Churches which are in missionary situations have not hesitated to use, under proper restraints, their right to excommunicate and this right has been occasionally and sparingly used in the British

Isles and in the U.S.A. But it has become part of the Anglican tradition that such measures are to be regarded as only a last resort in extreme cases; the constant use of ecclesiastical coercion, whether exercised through the bishops or not, is not an Anglican characteristic. Schooled by adversity, and not without the instruction of the Holy Spirit, the Anglican bishop prefers that his authority should be regarded basically as moral. It may well be that the climate of contemporary liberal democracy has exercised an influence here. But there are truths which God intends his Church to learn even from the *Zeitgeist*.

If we finally ask what are the peculiarly episcopal functions of an Anglican bishop, what are the things which he does that make an Anglican bishop a bishop, we must answer that he wields central representative authority in the Church, the authority of the Church and therefore the authority of Christ in the Church. When he ordains or takes part in a consecration he confers a permanent commission, trust, or responsibility, from God upon those whom he ordains for any holy office. Bishops do not constitute the Church, and they do not form a caste or order independent of the rest of the Church to which the inferior clergy and the laity are subordinated. Each bishop is a representative of the Church, within the Church, expressing its life and thought and actions. The bishop's position should be thought of as central rather than hierarchical. When a man is consecrated bishop, the consecrators lay their hands on his head, with all those who are present, clergy and laity, praying to God through Christ to ordain this man bishop. And in faith the Church believes that God through Christ does so ordain him. This is the act of the whole Church expressed through its proper duly appointed and authorized representatives, whose appointment is not merely *ad hoc* nor for the period of the functioning in a representative capacity, but permanent and life-long. And as the consecrated bishop is the Church's representative, so he is both the representative of the Church to God and necessarily therefore of God to the Church and in the Church to the world. He is not of course God's only means of encountering men nor of ruling his Church, but in those things in which he acts with authority he acts with God's authority.

The bishop's authority need be neither despotic nor absolute. He can and often does share and delegate his authority. He can and often does submit to constitutional restraints. And his authority, if he is true to Anglican tradition, will be pastoral rather than sacerdotal (though the two are not incompatible), moral, and as far as may be personal rather than legal. But the bishop must be *central*. The ancient Celtic ecclesiastical polity, in which bishops were often deprived of central authority and kept as mere ordaining officers, was a corruption of episcopacy. The bishop must be the centre of the Church. He is a representative concentration of the Church. He is the centre of the Church's authority in ordaining and confirming in his diocese. He ought to be the central liturgical authority. He must be the central authority in doctrine and tradition. He may of course take advice from theologians and other experts, lay and clerical, about doctrines and rites, but if he is to be true to the pattern of early episcopacy, the Anglican bishop must regard himself as pre-eminently the guardian of tradition in his diocese, and, with his fellow-bishops, in the Church at large. A bishop who does not know, and does not attempt to discover, what sort of doctrine the clergy in his diocese are preaching and teaching is failing his duty. It is his business above all to know what Christianity is about and to see that it is properly preserved, interpreted, applied, and handed on. The bishop ought to be a listener as well as a speaker, a teacher as well as an administrator. It is his responsibility to see that the Word of God has free course in his diocese. In this necessity both Scripture and tradition unite.

9

Oversight and Discipline

BERNARD PAWLEY

Arguments commending the acceptance of episcopacy to Churches or communities which do not possess it too rarely give chief consideration to the belief that *episcope* is a *charisma*. The good ordering of the Church requires that those who, under God, are endowed with qualities of leadership should be carefully chosen, set aside, and entrusted with a certain amount of authority in the name of the Lord and for the edifying of the Church. Patriarchs, judges, kings, prophets, apostles, all showed forth in some way or other the varied qualities of leadership with which it pleased the Lord to endow his Church. The new covenant does not enjoin the discontinuance of leadership: it sets a new pattern for its exercise. The normal embodiment of this charisma, in most places and throughout most ages of the Christian era, has been the office of bishop. The chief function of the *episcopos*, be he bishop, moderator, presbyter, church president, or what you will, is to act as head to the several members; to prevent any of the "diversities of administration" getting the upper hand. The pastor, the evangelist, the theologian, the canon lawyer, the ascetic, the administrator (in the modern sense), the moralist, and the rest can be an unruly crowd. The pages of church history are studded with the tragedies which result when one or more of these charismata are allowed undue prominence and hold the rest in restraint. Sometimes it is the *episcopos* himself who becomes intolerable. The Churches of the Reformation eventually had to throw off the pope because, as a governmental system, he failed to work; but then most of them made the opposite mistake of elevating the theologian on principle to the bishop's throne, thus getting all the other functions out of joint. Sometimes the zeal of the evangelist has burst the bonds and overthrown good government, so that in the long run his only achievement (contrary to his original inspiration) has been to form a new sect or denomination, which in its turn has settled down to formal uninspired existence.

Modern Roman Catholicism, at least since the First Vatican Council, has demonstrated both the evils and the strength of administration. But at last, in the middle of the twentieth century, the day of the administrator, in his formidable alliance with the canon lawyer, had come to an end. The pastor and the liberating theologian joined forces to overthrow this deadly combination, and so the Second Vatican Council, aided by the Pope himself, has gone a long way to restore *episcope* to the bishops. We have been able to compliment the Church of Rome on her return to the camp of episcopal Churches after her centuries of papal captivity.

Christendom's most recent outburst, Pentecostalism, is the evangelist's violent attempt to overthrow an arid combination of theologian and administrator which had been responsible for so much inertia in Protestant Churches. But it is reported that Pentecostalism itself is already in search of some sort of oversight and discipline. Somebody has to organize the debate as to whether Pentecostalist ministers should, or should not, have theological training. The episode of the "New Theology" provides yet another illustration of the true function of *episcope*, or rather of the evils attendant on the lack of it. For here the theologian has rightly revolted against the catechist's failure to come abreast of the twentieth century when dealing with the "image" of God. But the lack of effective *episcope* over it has allowed the theological revolution to cause distress and dismay by overstatement. The task of making the theologian the servant, rather than the tyrant, of the Church while allowing him adequate liberty to exercise his *charisma*, is always one of the most difficult functions of oversight. For the *cathedra* belongs not to the professor, but to the bishop. The real "doctor in divinity" is not necessarily the professional expert in academical divinity, but the *episcopos* who is responsible for the dissemination of the truth in such a manner as will edify.

Part of the task of ecumenism is to rebuild a centre of oversight and discipline, of overall *episcope*. Protestantism in fragmentation is often at the mercy of the theologians, and the recovery of unity is consequently regarded too often as an academic exercise. The World Council of Churches and its committees is by its very nature and constitution dominated by secretaries, that is, by departmental experts. *Episcope*, when the time comes to reconstruct it at the world level, must consist much more of the function of a chairman than of a secretary, as those terms are normally understood.

These few instances tend to the conclusion that *episcope* in good order, working naturally, is seen to be an essential function of, a necessary *charisma* in, God's household, if the headship of Christ and the inspiration of the Holy Spirit are to find effective expression within it. This does not prejudge the form which *episcope* may take, for the received order of bishops in a threefold ministry is only one of the possible solutions. But it is hard to deny that some form of bishop-in-presbytery, with built-in participation of the laity, is now the pragmatical way forward.

Before this *episcope* can be firmly established, can function well and command respect, there are certain fundamental assumptions prevailing (some would call them prejudices) which need deep examination. The worst of these is the prejudice that there is some necessary antagonism between the law and the gospel, that good order in the Church is a hindrance to the free passage of the Spirit. In England at least, there are large numbers of churchmen who would regard any form of discipline for the laity as "legalistic" or "rigorist" and would assume that what they call the "pastoral approach" implies the total absence of effective regulation. The second (which is also strong in England) is that good order is "High Church" and therefore suspect as "Romanism", while free discipline is more in the nature of the "Free Churches", and therefore "Low Church". But yet a quick examination will show that church discipline is much "higher" in the Presbyterian Churches than in the Episcopalian. An American Methodist bishop's function is very much closer to that of the pope than that of any Episcopalian (and, in practice, than that of many a "reformed" Roman Catholic bishop). It is to be hoped that prejudices under both these heads will be removed and a new understanding of the use and function of good order (which implies a body of flexible canon law) will be widely commended throughout the Church. Responsible discipline, firmly administered and gladly received, is a clear principle of the Scriptures.

The Anglican Communion is in a particular difficulty because the Lambeth Conference has no canonical authority, and as the Ecumenical Movement is now developing it does not look as though it can now acquire such authority. On the other hand, for *episcope* to gain respect locally it must be seen to have some international sanction. The Anglican Communion should therefore beware of being responsible for the creation of totally independent national (if not nationalist) Churches, unless it is at the same time at pains to build up the kind of international consensus which so obviously gives strength and respect to the Roman episcopate.

The episcopal office, as exercised in the provinces of Canterbury and York, is probably further from the ideal of the episcopate than any other, except perhaps the Roman titular bishop consecrated to sit in a Vatican departmental armchair, which is the nadir. But the English bishop works under difficulties. Appointed by the State (no degree of "consultations" can alter the hard fact), he is expected to exercise the *episcope* without most of its powers. It was an English bishop who said that for him *episcopos* should be translated "onlooker". Without a curia, without control of his cathedral, without a synod, he has limited powers of patronage and little effective jurisdiction. Finance, pastoral reorganization, education, missionary strategy, even now the selection and training of ordinands, are all in effect out of his hands. Effective oversight is made impossible by the size of dioceses and by the necessary preoccupation of the bishop (still) in ecclesiastical and civil affairs on a national scale. Discipline is rendered impossible by freehold of the clergy (which is as much a "mentality" as a legal right) and by the general unwillingness of Anglican laity in England to accept any discipline whatsoever. This latter difficulty is ministered to by a strangely persistent misinterpretation of the function of a "national Church" whereby it is assumed that all citizens, as such, whether of any religious persuasion or none, have a right to all its benefits without question and without qualification. Recent debates on the resumption of the canon law have shown that there is a deep-rooted acceptance of this whole position in both Church and nation. And it is clear that only a radical change of the "establishment" can bring any improvement. It is to be hoped that the new world, once more, will be called in to redress the balance of the old. The "Partners in Ministry" report does at least point a way forward. The Synodical Government idea without it must be a dead letter.

Every Anglican should be inspired to the renewal of the episcopate by the experience of the Church of South India. The Church of England at the Reformation evidently started out in the hope of such renewal. Cranmer, in the *Reformatio legum ecclesiasticarum*, provides that the bishop should summon a synod each year "to discuss all matters pertaining to the profit and well-being of the people of

God". The Lambeth Appeal to all Christian people, four centuries later, still had to express the "desire that the office of a bishop should be everywhere exercised in a representative and constitutional manner". It would be stimulating if the Lambeth Conference of 1968 were to call upon those provinces where this is still not implemented (are there any besides Canterbury and York?) to institute reforms forthwith.

One of the important functions of "oversight" by the bishop is the communication to his subordinates of the overall picture of Christ's work in the world and in the diocese which he alone is in a position to see. Each pastor is immersed in the work and concerns of his own cure; but the bishop is liberated from momentary local cares in order to be able to take the broader prospect. But having taken it, from his privileged position, he is under obligation to communicate his findings. This oversight carries with it responsibility for planning the work of the team, and, of course, the pastoral care of the flock, both clerical and lay. *Accipe curam meam ac tuam* has lost its real impact, at least in England, because induction to a cure of souls does, in fact, invest an incumbent with absolute powers with which the bishop is not expected to interfere. Real effective episcopal "visitation" does not exist. The rigidity of the parochial system, the freehold and the existence of patronage makes corporate *episcope* very difficult, but in the new united episcopal Churches a new and exciting relationship is being worked out. There are parts of the Communion where the possibility of episcopal task-force projects is being canvassed. Enthusiasts for this form of episcopate are naturally overfaced by the absurdity of being called "*the* bishop" *of* some immense country in which there are already some hundreds of (Roman Catholic) residential bishops. But the situation of such a bishop is not so peculiar as might at first be thought. In the "post-Christian" era all bishops are increasingly becoming leaders of minority task forces. It will not be long before the Pope himself will be able to be described as "the Bishop *in* Rome". The designation of a territorial area does not assign pastoral responsibility for all citizens within it, but only first for the baptized confessional adherents. Beyond that it would be open to a bishop to initiate any kind of scheme or team project in the area.

It is strange that the Roman Church is more relaxed about parallel episcopates than the Anglican Communion. It is not generally realized that there are many parallel episcopal jurisdictions in Italy itself; and indeed several in the large cities of the U.S.A. But the Roman Church is more effectively held together by unity of belief and by authoritative discipline, and can therefore afford to be less rigid about the territorial responsibilities of the bishops.

These disjointed remarks about oversight must return to where they began, at the oversight of doctrine and teaching. The recovery of good order must involve some responsibility for the preservation and constant renewal of *orthē doxa*. This is an unpopular suggestion at a time when theologians are questioning the very possibility of creeds, let alone of right ones. The agonized cry of the New York vestryman who, after a Sunday of being told that his conception of God was in need of renewal, asked, "Well, what in hell do they want me to believe?—I'm sick of being told that what they taught me twenty five years ago is all washed up", is uttering a real censure of the episcopate. One of the chief sources of weakness in contemporary Christian life is the fact that the normal "believer" is bombarded by new currents of faith, order, life, and work which are totally unrelated. "Christian atheism", uncontrolled, unco-ordinated, sparks off, naturally enough, fundamentalist, salvationist evangelism. The task for episcopates of all kinds is perhaps most clearly seen in South America where the *pontifices* (bridge-builders indeed!) are called upon to show how new Roman Catholic liberalism, Pentecostalism, and extreme Protestant evangelism are all winds of the same Spirit blowing for renewal. When bishops of the Roman obedience are gladly releasing their imprisoned theologians from the shackles of centuries, and when the multitudinous non-Roman shepherds are beginning to protect their sheep from the derangement which might be caused by exposure to the blasts of every vain doctrine, they might find themselves meeting in the middle of a pastoral no-man's-land, where the pasture is richer than they thought.

All the foregoing reflections imply that we have at last got over some of the more violent reactions of the Reformation—against spiritual and doctrinal tyranny—and that we can now address ourselves to sober thought on good order in the Church as regards oversight. Can the same hopes be entertained about discipline? Or does the sale of Indulgences still cast too long a shadow over Europe and America? In that case we shall have to hope that once again the new Churches, who will be free from the inbuilt prejudices of the West, will show us the way. For many Protestants, the very word "discipline" conjures up notions of the schoolmaster, the boy, and the birch, which seem far from the patterns of the gospel. But their Bibles should relate discipline to discipleship and turn their thoughts to yokes which are easy, to burdens which are light, and to crosses which have to be carried cheerfully for the gospel's sake. Anglican Churches have had to fight uphill against the harm done by the Mother Church's experience as the national Church. In Britain, the belief that all citizens are Christians, and are all entitled to the ministrations of the Church, has made total havoc of baptism discipline and so of every other form of order. The persistence of unregulated infant baptism means that church membership carries with it no *differentiae* at all. In England, at least, the baptized Anglican, as such, recognizes no Christian responsibilities and cannot be distinguished from his unbaptized neighbour. This, in turn, makes it difficult to exercise any marriage discipline or to do anything about funerals, except to minister Christian burial without differentiation. The effects of this on those who stand outside and observe are most discouraging —are a "scandal" in the New Testament sense.

The abolition of a discipline of penitence at the Reformation has had disastrous consequences. The average Anglican, at least in the older nations—let us not avoid the unpleasant conclusion—does not repent, has no systematic penitence. Generations of "general confession" have not served him well. The restoration of "discipleship-discipline" demands ingenuity in this field. What system can be devised whereby the Christian is brought face to face regularly with the fact of sin and so to a knowledge of grace and forgiveness? Is it surprising that there is a recrudescence of "holiness" sects who call themselves "Christians", with the implication that the non-penitent, formalized, church members have forfeited the right to that title?

Discipline of service has been attempted in stewardship campaigns, without spectacular results. Has God raised up the disciplined bands of Mormon youth, consecrated to two years' overseas witness *in virtue of church membership*, to rebuke our apathy?

The chaos of marriage practice throughout the Protestant world has made the solution of the mixed marriage problem almost insoluble on a world scale for the Roman Catholic Church. How can they be expected to commit themselves? Is there adequate instruction before marriage? Is our teaching consistent? But the most shaming consideration of all is this, that, for example in England, it can be shown that only one in twenty of Anglicans gives his children *any religious upbringing at all*. So is it to be wondered that the Roman

Church at least tries to secure that the children have some religious education? Is there not room for discipleship responsibility here?

How many Anglicans can be said to be adequately prepared for death? The provisions of the 1662 book are no longer usable. Troops in the recent war commented frequently on the inadequacy of our ministry at this point in comparison with the professional competence of the Roman priest. It was the ordered discipleship that impressed.

The calling forth of willing "discipleship-discipline" duly regulated is a clamant need for Anglican Christians, and it should be a primary claim on the time of the Lambeth overseers. The lack of it has done much harm. It need not, in fact would not, stifle legitimate freedom and diversity. The oversight would have to be not of constraint but willing (1 Pet.5.2). There is much good will to be enlisted. Discipleship of money has already caused some to look deeper into other forms of stewardship. There are signs that even in Britain a certain amount of gentle regulation, if it could be seen to come from authority properly constituted, would not be unwelcome. The episcopates of the new nations are having to build up the pattern of the Christian life from nothing. Much of their experience could help the shepherds of the Christian remnants in the old world.

Acknowledgement

Thanks are due to the following for permission to quote from copyright sources:

C.M.S. News Letter (January 1966): Dr Taylor's editorial.